THE SHOOTING SCRIPT®

CAPOTE

SCREENPLAY BY DAN FUTTERMAN
BASED ON THE BOOK BY GERALD CLARKE

FOREWORD BY GERALD CLARKE

A Newmarket Shooting Script® Series Book

NEWMARKET PRESS • NEW YORK

FIRST EDITION

10   9   8   7   6   5   4   3   2   1

ISBN-13: 978-1-55704-723-6
ISBN-10: 1-55704-723-5

Library of Congress Catalog-in-Publication Data available upon request.

QUANTITY PURCHASES

Companies, professional groups, clubs, and other organizations may qualify for special terms when ordering quantities
of this title. For information, write to Special Sales, Newmarket Press, 18 East 48th Street, New York, NY 10017;
call (212) 832-3575 or 1-800-669-3903; FAX (212) 832-3629; or e-mail info@newmarketpress.com.
Website: www.newmarketpress.com
Manufactured in the United States of America.

OTHER BOOKS IN THE NEWMARKET SHOOTING SCRIPT® SERIES INCLUDE:

About a Boy: The Shooting Script	*I ♥ Huckabees: The Shooting Script*
Adaptation: The Shooting Script	*The Ice Storm: The Shooting Script*
The Age of Innocence: The Shooting Script	*In Good Company: The Shooting Script*
American Beauty: The Shooting Script	*A Knight's Tale: The Shooting Script*
Ararat: The Shooting Script	*Man on the Moon: The Shooting Script*
A Beautiful Mind: The Shooting Script	*The Matrix: The Shooting Script*
Big Fish: The Shooting Script	*The People vs. Larry Flynt: The Shooting Script*
The Birdcage: The Shooting Script	*Pieces of April: The Shooting Script*
Black Hawk Down: The Shooting Script	*Punch-Drunk Love: The Shooting Script*
Cast Away: The Shooting Script	*Red Dragon: The Shooting Script*
Cinderella Man: The Shooting Script	*The Shawshank Redemption: The Shooting Script*
The Constant Gardener: The Shooting Script	*Sideways: The Shooting Script*
Dead Man Walking: The Shooting Script	*Snow Falling on Cedars: The Shooting Script*
Eternal Sunshine of the Spotless Mind:	*The Squid and the Whale: The Shooting Script*
The Shooting Script	*State and Main: The Shooting Script*
Gods and Monsters: The Shooting Script	*Traffic: The Shooting Script*
Gosford Park: The Shooting Script	*The Truman Show: The Shooting Script*
Human Nature: The Shooting Script	*War of the Worlds: The Shooting Script*

OTHER NEWMARKET PICTORIAL MOVIEBOOKS AND NEWMARKET INSIDER FILM BOOKS INCLUDE:

Amistad: A Celebration of the Film by Steven Spielberg	*Frida: Bringing Frida Kahlo's Life and Art to Film**
The Art of The Matrix*	*Gladiator: The Making of the Ridley Scott Epic Film*
The Art of X2*	*Hotel Rwanda: Bringing the True Story of an African Hero to Film**
Catch Me If You Can: The Illustrated Screenplay*	*The Jaws Log*
Chicago: The Movie and Lyrics*	*Kinsey: Public and Private**
Cold Mountain: The Journey from Book to Film	*Ray: A Tribute to the Movie, the Music, and the Man**
Dances with Wolves: The Illustrated Story of the Epic Film*	*Saving Private Ryan: The Men, The Mission, The Movie*
E. T. The Extra-Terrestrial: From Concept to Classic—The	*Schindler's List: Images of the Steven Spielberg Film*
Illustrated Story of the Film and the Filmmakers*	

* Includes Screenplay

CONTENTS

FOREWORD

GERALD CLARKE

Like all American writers, Truman Capote loved the movies. But Capote's relationship with films was, from an early age, unusually intimate. It began in the years just before World War II when he led his teenage friends on weekend expeditions to the Pickwick Theater in Greenwich, Connecticut. Emboldened—and perhaps inspired—by hidden bottles of sweet brandy, they took vigorous part in the on-screen drama, laughing when they were supposed to cry, crying when they were supposed to laugh, and, until they were kicked out by angry ushers, substituting their own dialogue for the words coming out of the actors' mouths.

A little over a decade later, in the early fifties, Capote was the one putting the words into those mouths. Living in Italy with his companion, Jack Dunphy, he was recruited by David O. Selznick, the producer of *Gone with the Wind*, to write some new lines for Montgomery Clift and Selznick's wife, Jennifer Jones, to speak in *Indiscretion of an American Wife*, a film Selznick was making in Rome with Vittorio De Sica, one of the masters of Italian neorealism.

Capote's contribution to that awkwardly titled film was small, but Selznick was so impressed by his innovative dialogue that he recommended him to John Huston, who was about to direct his own movie in Italy. "His is, in my opinion, one of the freshest and *most original* and most exciting writing talents of our time," Selznick wrote Huston. "And what he would say through these characters, and how he would have them say it, would be so completely different from anything that has been heard from a motion picture theater's sound box as to also give you something completely fresh—or so at least I think."

The making of *Beat the Devil* could make a movie itself—and someday probably will. The backdrop of the Amalfi coast in chilly February. A cast that includes Humphrey Bogart, Jennifer Jones, Gina Lollobrigida, and Robert

Morley. And Truman Capote, wearing an overcoat that fell almost to his ankles, with a long lavender scarf flapping behind it, rushing down to the set every morning with dialogue he had spent the night writing. But Selznick was right. Capote did provide the movie's characters with words that were completely fresh. For me, and for many others, *Beat the Devil* is a small comic masterpiece, as original now as it was in 1953.

In the years that followed, Capote wrote other screenplays, most notably *The Innocents* (1961), which was an adaptation of Henry James's *The Turn of the Screw*. By the mid-seventies, Capote and his idiosyncrasies—his childlike voice and his flamboyant personality—were so famous that Neil Simon modeled a comic villain after him in his mystery farce, *Murder by Death* (1976). When the time came to cast the picture, one of Simon's colleagues had an inspiration. Instead of getting someone *like* Truman Capote to play the villain, he asked, why not get Truman Capote himself?

Truman was thrilled. All American writers may love the movies, but how many of them are actually given a chance to star in one? The excitement soon evaporated, and when I visited him on the set in Burbank, Truman was miserable—anxious and exhausted. Acting, as he should have known, requires unseemly early hours, hard work, and a talent he did not possess. When the cameras rolled, Truman Capote was not a very good Truman Capote.

After Truman's death in 1984, a few more Capote-like characters wafted across the screen. Truman is an irresistible subject for scriptwriters, but few of them have looked beyond his peculiarities; until now they have turned him into a parody of the man I wrote about. The Truman Capote I knew was more than a collection of witticisms and effeminate gestures. He was, in fact, the most complicated and contradictory person I've ever met.

"I won't respect you unless you tell the whole truth," Truman told me when I began my biography, and I followed his directive as best I could, giving a full account of his faults, as well as his virtues. The whole truth is what I wanted in any movie made of his life. And that was my chief concern when Danny Futterman first approached me with a draft of his script and introduced me to the team that was to create a movie based on my biography.

Danny and Bennett Miller, *Capote*'s director, have known each other since they were boys of twelve in the northern suburbs of New York. Philip Seymour Hoffman, who plays Capote, became their friend a few years later at a summer drama camp. Until I met them I didn't know such institutions existed. When other boys were batting balls or shooting baskets, Danny, Bennett, and Phil were learning how to be actors, directors, and scriptwriters—the Hardy Boys in search of adventure in Hollywood and on Broadway. Nancy Drew joined the trio some years later in the form of Caroline Baron, *Capote*'s producer.

If I wanted the movie to tell the truth about Capote, so, I soon discovered, did they. By *truth* I don't mean a literal retelling of my biography, which covers Capote's entire life of nearly sixty years. *Capote*, the movie, by contrast, centers on only a few chapters of my book, those that tell the story of the five years he spent researching and writing *In Cold Blood*. But Danny's instinct to concentrate on the *In Cold Blood* years was both right and necessary.

Though the frame was thus reduced to only a few years of Capote's life, many elements, people, and events still had to be left out, and time had to be compressed. In real life, for example, Truman and Harper Lee, who helped with his research, did not leave for Kansas until a few weeks after he read the report of the Clutter killings. In the movie, they board a train just a few hours after he puts down the newspaper—indeed, that very night. Complications were simplified, and dialogue, such as the interchange between Capote and Lee aboard the train, was invented.

Truman Capote in Milan negotiating a contract for the Italian edition of *In Cold Blood*, February 1, 1966.

Keystone/Getty Images

All that was fine by me. A movie—a good movie, anyway—is a drama, not a documentary, and dramas are works of art that must be contained and shaped. The reality I wanted to convey was not a list of petty details. It was the real truth about Truman Capote: that beneath his sometimes frivolous exterior, he was an artist—one of the best writers of his generation.

My role, then, was to help this quartet of talented filmmakers find the essence of Truman Capote. They had questions, and I had answers. I had questions, and they had answers. Danny dubbed me the Consigliere. Bennett called me the Enforcer. I like both titles, but I prefer to think of myself as the Guide, the man who led them through a tangled life and a time, the early sixties, before they were born. One of my corrections was to inform them that in those days, profanity was less common than it is now. Back then, most people had a wider command of useful adjectives than they do today, and certain four-letter words, now heard on every street corner, were confined to army barracks.

What would Truman—Truman the moviegoer, Truman the movie scriptwriter, and Truman the movie actor—have thought about this movie that bears his name? I wonder myself. I do know, however, that those who made it have followed his instructions to me. They have done their very best to tell the truth.

CAPOTE

by
Dan Futterman

Based on the book "Capote: A Biography" by
Gerald Clarke

Shooting Script
August 30, 2004

TITLE UP: "Western Kansas, 1959"

1   **EXT. FARMHOUSE - MORNING**   1

    The CAMERA follows a SIXTEEN YEAR OLD GIRL, long hair, pretty
    Sunday church dress, walking toward a peaceful farmhouse. At
    the door she lifts the knocker. The door opens slightly.
    The girl turns and looks past the camera at her MOTHER,
    sitting in an old Plymouth idling in the driveway. Her
    mother shrugs, motions for her to go inside.

2   **INT. FARMHOUSE - CONTINUOUS**   2

    The girl walks through the downstairs rooms. In the kitchen,
    the PHONE is OFF the hook. The girl looks back toward the
    open front door. She turns toward the stairs, climbs them.

3   **INT. FARMHOUSE, UPSTAIRS HALL - CONTINUOUS**   3

    She walks down the hall to a BEDROOM DOOR at the end. The
    door is slightly ajar. She knocks, then enters the room.

4   **INT. FARMHOUSE, BEDROOM - CONTINUOUS**   4

    The girl's POV: the CAMERA pans across the bedroom of a high
    school coed. We see the desk, the bureau, the bed. On the
    bed lies NANCY CLUTTER, her wrists and legs bound in rope,
    SHOT in the head. There is blood on the wall. The sixteen
    year-old girl stands immobile. Before she starts to scream,

                                   CUT TO:

EXT. KANSAS LANDSCAPE - DAY

    Trees ring the edge of a field.

                                     CUT TO:

5   **EXT. N.Y. CITYSCAPE, ESTABLISHING - NIGHT**   5

    Buildings lit against the night sky.

6   INT. NEW YORK APARTMENT BUILDING/STAIRS - NIGHT   6

    Camera follows group of partygoers as they mount the stairs:
    Truman Capote, Barbara (very tall), Rose, Christopher,
    Williams.

INT. SMALL, PACKED NEW YORK APARTMENT/KITCHEN - LATER

The friends are standing in the crowded kitchen - people are
coming in and out - talking and drinking and laughing.

                    TRUMAN
          So Jimmy Baldwin tells me the plot
          of his book, and he says to me: the
          writing's going well, but I just
          want to make sure it's not one of
          those problem novels. I said:
          Jimmy, your novel's about a Negro
          homosexual who's in love with a Jew
          - wouldn't you call that a problem?

Laughter.

                    CHRISTOPHER
          Susan's father had a minor heart
          attack, so she's writing more
          erotic poems about death and sex.

                    BARBARA
          It's so tiresome.

                    WILLIAMS
          Hmm. What rhymes with angina?

Laughter. We see Truman watching everyone laugh. GRAYSON
notices, leans in to him. As the rest of the group continues
talking, we come closer, hear their conversation.

                    GRAYSON
          How's your writing?

                    TRUMAN
          Oh, I've got a million ideas of
          what to write next - I just have to
          choose one.

                    GRAYSON
          Really?

                    TRUMAN
          No.

Their attention is pulled back into the group as:

                    BARBARA
          Who would I want to play me?
          Natalie Wood.

                    ROSE
Too fat.

                    BARBARA
Audrey Hepburn?

                    ROSE
Not bad. Sort of middle-class.

                    TRUMAN
When a movie is made of my life I
know exactly who I want as me...
          (beat)
Marilyn Monroe.

Barbara cracks up, chokes on her drink.

6   EXT. TRUMAN AND JACK'S HOUSE/BACK PATIO - MORNING   6

Truman sits with his coffee, reading the New York Times. An
article catches his eye. He sits up straight, folds the
paper over, reads it.

6   **INT. TRUMAN AND JACK'S HOUSE, STUDY - DAY**   6

C/U of article being snipped out of PAGE 39 of the Times,
November 16, 1959. As the page gets turned around with each
snip, we see a small PHOTO of a middle-aged man wearing
glasses, with the caption: "FOUND DEAD: Herbert W. Clutter, a
wealthy Kansas farmer...." We read the headline: "WEALTHY
FARMER, 3 OF FAMILY SLAIN. Parts of the story: "HOLCOMB,
Kan., Nov. 15 (UPI) - ... wheat farmer, his wife ...two young
children found shot today...."

INT. TRUMAN AND JACK'S HOUSE, STUDY - MOMENTS LATER

Truman on the phone.

                    FEMALE VOICE OVER THE PHONE
New Yorker magazine.

                    TRUMAN (ON PHONE)
William Shawn, please.
          (he listens)
Adorable one? All of a sudden I
know what article I'm going to
write for you next.

INT. TRUMAN AND JACK'S HOUSE, STUDY/KITCHEN - MOMENTS LATER

Truman on the phone, on a long cord, travels between the
study and the kitchen as he talks to William Shawn. We hear
pieces of the conversation, and see Truman in different parts
of the room as he says each bit.

> TRUMAN (ON PHONE)
> ... never had *anything* like this
> happen to them before. They're
> used to sleeping at night with the
> doors unlatched.... (laughs) Yes,
> we should buy stock in Master Locks-
> all of Kansas will be in the
> hardware store tomorrow.

Jump to -

> TRUMAN (ON PHONE)
> They have no idea who the killer
> is. But it doesn't *matter* who the
> killer is -- what matters is who
> the townspeople *imagine* the killer
> is. That's what I want to write
> about.

Jump to -

> TRUMAN (ON PHONE)
> I'm gonna need some help.... I'm
> thinking about Nelle - she can
> protect me....

JACK DUNPHY (strong, Irish-American, ten years older than
Truman) - his longtime boyfriend - enters the front door with
a bag of groceries, stops in the hall. He sees Truman on the
phone. Truman looks at Jack, though he's still speaking to
Shawn -

> TRUMAN (ON PHONE)
> I want to leave tonight...

                                        SMASH CUT TO:

7   **EXT. TRAIN TRACKS, OUTSKIRTS OF NEW YORK CITY - NIGHT**   7

A train barrels toward us, its headlight bright. The train
roars past, away from the city.

8   **INT. TRAIN, MOVING - NIGHT**   8

Truman hurries through the train, checking his ticket with
the sleeper cabins. His long SCARF trails behind. His
longer cashmere COAT practically brushes the floor.

9   **INT. TRUMAN AND HARPER LEE'S CABIN, TRAIN - CONTINUOUS**   9

Truman opens the door. Inside the cabin his childhood friend
from Monroeville, Alabama, NELLE HARPER LEE (yes, that Harper
Lee), is reading. She looks up, deadpan -

                    NELLE
          I figured you'd missed it.

Nelle is a year younger than Truman, dowdy in dress, but
smart, tough, sensible. Truman smiles.

                    TRUMAN
          God I'm glad you agreed to come.

                    TRUMAN
          You're the only one I know with the
          qualifications to be both a
          research assistant and personal
          bodyguard.
               (then, noticing)
          Oh, Nelle, you poor thing.

He tries to spruce up her limp silk scarf.

                    NELLE
          Off. Truman. Off.
               (holds his hands)
          I'm happy to see you too, but I can
          still whip your behind.

TWO BLACK PORTERS enter, one with an enormous TRUNK
(Truman's), the other with a sensible SUITCASE (Nelle's).

                    PORTER #1
               (reading tags)
          Mr. Truman Capote, Miss Nelle
          Harper Lee. Where would you like
          these, sir?

                    TRUMAN
          That one up there and that one on
          the floor.

He tips them.

                         NELLE
               What all did you bring?

                         PORTER #2
               Thank you greatly, sir. It's an
               honor to have you with us. If you
               don't mind my saying, your last
               book was even better than the first-

                         TRUMAN
               You're sweet.

                         PORTER #2
               Just when you think they've gotten
               as good as they can get.

                         TRUMAN
               Thank you. You're very kind.

                         PORTER #1
                    (to Nelle)
               Ma'am.

The PORTERS leave. Nelle is stunned. Truman fiddles with
the trunk locks, his back to Nelle. Silence, then:

                         NELLE
               You're pathetic.

Truman doesn't answer.

                         NELLE (cont'd)
               You're pathetic.

                         TRUMAN
               What?

                         NELLE
               You paid them to say that.

Truman won't look at her. She whacks him.

                         NELLE (cont'd)
               You paid them to say that!

                         TRUMAN
                    (squealing)
               How'd you know? How did you know?!

                         NELLE
               "Just when you think they've gotten
               as good as they can get."

                         TRUMAN
              You think that was too much?
                   (laughter)
              I thought that was a good line.

    More laughter. More smacking of Truman. Then it is quiet.

                         NELLE
              Pathetic.

9A   **INT. TRUMAN AND HARPER LEE'S CABIN, TRAIN - MORNING**   9A

     Nelle's awake, but still in her bunk, looking out the window
     at the Kansas plains. Truman's dressing, watching her.

                                                      CUT TO:

11   **EXT. COUNTRYSIDE - DAY**   11

     TRAVELING SHOTS of harvested FIELDS, grazing LIVESTOCK,
     solitary FARMHOUSES.

     The TRAIN chugs across the Kansas flatlands.

     SHOTS of SIGNS outside Garden City: "World's Largest Free
     Swimpool" and "Howdy, Stranger! Welcome to Garden City. A
     Friendly Place."

12   **EXT. GARDEN CITY RENT-A-CAR - DAY**   12

     Truman and Nelle rent a car. People stare.

13   **I/E. RENTAL CAR - DAY**   13

     Nelle drives past the main square, Truman in the passenger
     seat. Truman looks at a photo in THE GARDEN CITY TELEGRAM.

                         TRUMAN
              Alvin Dewey, Kansas Bureau of
              Investigation. KBI.

14   **INT. LOBBY, WALKER HOTEL, GARDEN CITY - DAY**   14

     Truman and Nelle check in. People stare. Nelle notices.

16   **EXT. FINNEY COUNTY COURTHOUSE, GARDEN CITY - CONTINUOUS**   16

     Truman and Nelle trot up the COURTHOUSE STEPS.

17   **INT. FINNEY COUNTY COURTHOUSE, LOBBY - MOMENTS LATER**   17

Truman approaches the GUARD DESK.

> TRUMAN
> Mr. Alvin Dewey, please.

> GUARD
> Third floor. In what used to be
> the Sheriff's Office.

Truman CURTSIES.

18   **INT. SHERIFF'S OFFICE - DAY**   18

In the reception area, ALVIN DEWEY and the two other KBI
AGENTS assigned to the Clutter case are getting their jackets
on and straightening their ties. They've completely taken
over the office. They are: HAROLD "Brother" NYE (34); and
ROY "Curly" CHURCH (60 - bald). They all smoke.

Sheriff WALTER SANDERSON - 60's, kind, overweight - is office-
less (though he and his wife DOROTHY still live on the fourth
floor of the Courthouse.) WALTER lurks in the background,
nowhere to go, emptying one of many FILLED ASHTRAYS, BOTHERED
by the SMOKE. Truman and Nelle enter as:

> CHURCH
> The wife said no more smoking in
> the house. I told her, "Fine.
> Walter's got a couch upstairs in
> his apartment. I'll stay with him
> and Dorothy till we're done here."
> (to Walter)
> I've got my bag and a carton of
> cigarettes in the car.

WALTER looks uncomfortable. Dewey shakes his head at Church.

> DEWEY
> Roy.

> TRUMAN
> Mr. Dewey. Truman Capote from the
> New Yorker.

Silence. The Agents stare at him.

> TRUMAN (cont'd)
> Hello.

Silence. Nye is looking at Truman, particularly puzzled.

                    TRUMAN (cont'd)
          Bergdorf's.

                    NYE
          Sorry?

                    TRUMAN
          The scarf.

                    NYE
          Oh.
               (then)
          Nice.

                    TRUMAN
          Thank you.
               (turns to Dewey)
          I wonder when we could arrange an
          interview? Some time to talk.

Dewey stubs out his cigarette.

                    DEWEY
          About what?

                    TRUMAN
          We're not looking for any inside
          information - I don't care one way
          or another if you catch whoever did
          this - I'm writing an article not
          about the Clutter killings, but how
          they're affecting the town, how you
          all are bearing up -

                    DEWEY
          I care.

                    TRUMAN
          Excuse me?

                    DEWEY
          I care.
               (puts on his hat, pulls
                out another cigarette)
          I care a great deal if we catch
          whoever did this.

                    TRUMAN
          Yes -

                    DEWEY
          As do a lot of folks around here.

                    TRUMAN
          Of course.

Dewey walks out. Nye and Church start out after him.

                    NYE
               (to Church)
          New Yorker?

                    CHURCH
          You have press credentials?

                    NYE
          What's the New Yorker?

                    CHURCH
          Magazine.

                    TRUMAN
          Magazines don't give out —

                    CHURCH
          You can come to the news conference
          with the rest of them.
               (tips his hat to Nelle)
          Sears and Roebuck.

Nelle and Truman are left alone.

INT. SPARE COURTROOM - DAY

Packed with PRESS from all over the Midwest, as well as local
Finney County CITIZENS.

Dewey's leading the press conference from a FOLDING TABLE set
up in front of the Judge's bench, flanked by the two other
KBI Agents. He's got a cigarette burning in an ashtray.
Truman and Nelle stand in the back.

                    DEWEY
          I'll talk facts but I won't
          speculate. The main fact here we
          need to be clear on is not one, but
          four people were killed. A lot of
          folks say Herb Clutter had to be
          the main target because he was
          dealt with the most brutally —

                    JOURNALIST #1
          Had his throat cut.

                    DEWEY
               (a moment)
          Yes. We'd all like to know why.
          But it could've been any one of the
          family they were after. We just
          don't know -

                    JOURNALIST #2
          You've identified the murder
          weapon?

                    DEWEY
          Wounds indicate a shotgun, close-
          range, but no casings were found.

                    JOURNALIST #1
          Twelve-gauge, hunting -

                    DEWEY
          Right.

                    JOURNALIST #1
          They were all shot in the face?

Dewey looks at the journalist. Then, evenly:

                    DEWEY
          No. Nancy in the back of the head.

                    JOURNALIST #2
          Is there any evidence of, I'm
          sorry, sexual molestation of the
          women?

                    DEWEY
          No.

                    JOURNALIST #2
          Anything else stolen?

                    DEWEY
          Kenyon's radio seems to be the
          only...

                    JOURNALIST #3
          The boy was sixteen?

                    DEWEY
          Fifteen. Nancy was sixteen.

                    JOURNALIST #2
          It's her friend that found them?

                       DEWEY
Laura Kinney.

                       JOURNALIST #2
Spell that?

                       DEWEY
I assume you're okay with the Laura
part. K-I-N-N-E-Y. But, please,
leave her be.

Lots of folks try to talk at once, one OLD MAN makes himself
heard above the rest:

                       OLD MAN
There's talk of a bunch of
Mexicans, a whole bunch of
Mexicans...

                       DEWEY
           (standing, stubs out
            cigarette)
George, it's good to see you again.
I do have an opinion whether this
was the work of one man or a whole
bunch, as you said, but it doesn't
matter a whole lot whether it was
Mexicans or Methodists or Eskimos.
We're going to find whoever did
this. Four good people from our
community are dead. Let's remember
that. Okay with you?
           (holds up a notice)
The West Kansas Farm Committee's
offering a thousand dollar reward
for information leading to an
arrest. Please print that.
           (moving to the exit)
Thank you all for coming.

The room is immediately noisy as Dewey makes his way to the
door, pulling a pack of cigarettes from his pocket, followed
by Church and Nye. He's about to step out when Truman
catches his eye. Dewey exits.

                                     CUT TO:

20   **INT. RENTAL CAR - LATE AFTERNOON**   20

Nelle drives while consulting a MAP. Truman is leaning back,
looking out at the passing farms through the window. He
speaks almost to himself.

                    TRUMAN
          Mr. Dewey's protective of the
          Clutters. I wonder how well he
          knew them...

Nelle glances over at him. He doesn't notice.

                    TRUMAN (cont'd)
          He was foxy with that old man.
               (turns to Nelle)
          Are you ever gonna let me drive?

                    NELLE
          Truman, you're a menace. You can
          barely see over the wheel.

Truman looks back out the window at the farms, leans back.

                    NELLE (cont'd)
          This make you miss Alabama?

                    TRUMAN
               (rolling window down,
                shakes his head)
          Not even a little bit.

He leans his head out, closes his eyes.

21   **EXT. CLUTTER FARM - SUNSET**   21

     Nelle pulls their car to the side of the COUNTY ROAD which
     fronts the CLUTTER FARM. We recognize the FARMHOUSE as the
     one in which Nancy Clutter was found dead. A HIGHWAY
     PATROLMAN (20 years old) sits in a CRUISER parked up the
     driveway.

     CRIME SCENE TAPE marks the perimeter of the property. Truman
     and Nelle get out of their car, stand at the foot of the
     driveway, gazing at the lonely farmhouse.

                                             FADE OUT.

22   **EXT. HOLCOMB HIGH SCHOOL - MORNING**   22

     A gorgeous fall day. Crowds of kids arriving at school. Many
     are SOMBER. As Truman and Nelle walk toward the kids, some
     look warily at Truman and give him a wide berth.

                    TRUMAN
          Hello.

Kids back away. Nelle notices. She leaves Truman, walks up
to a group of THREE GIRLS.

                    NELLE
          Morning.

                    GIRL #1
          Hi.

                    NELLE
          Can any of you tell me where I'd
          find Laura Kinney?

                    GIRL #1
          Oh, um...

The girl glances toward the school entrance where LAURA
KINNEY (who found Nancy Clutter's body) walks with DANNY
BURKE (tall, 17).

                    NELLE
              (gently)
          Is that her? With the tall boy?

                    GIRL #2
          Yeah. With Danny Burke.

                    NELLE
          Danny Burke?
              (Girl #2 nods)
          Thank you.

As Nelle leaves, Girl #1 turns to her friend:

                    GIRL #2
          Oh, quiet yourself, Janice.

Nelle sees Truman on his way toward Laura, calls out -

                    NELLE
          Truman. Truman -

Truman doesn't hear. She watches Truman approach them.
Laura backs away. Danny leads her off. Nelle walks over to
Truman, looks at him for several moments.

                    NELLE (cont'd)
          These folks live their lives in a
          particular way. You need to
          consider adapting yourself to that
          fact.

                    TRUMAN
          What -

                    NELLE
          - I'm gonna find out where those
          two kids live. Maybe you'll let me
          do that alone?

Nelle leaves. On Truman, as the bell rings and the mass of
teenagers starts to enter the school.

                                        CUT TO:

23 **EXT. MAIN STREET, GARDEN CITY - DAY**   23

     Truman walks alone, sees the Gilbart Funeral Home. He
     removes his hat, slips past the few people standing outside.

24 **INT. GILBART FUNERAL HOME - CONTINUOUS**   24

     Warm but slightly tacky. Some people are engaged in hushed
     conversation at the reception area. Truman slips past, into
     the back room.

25 **INT. BACK ROOM, GILBART FUNERAL HOME - CONTINUOUS**   25

     No people, low light. Four CLOSED CASKETS at the back of the
     room. Truman walks over slowly. After a moment, he checks
     to make sure he's alone. Then he LIFTS THE TOP of one of the
     caskets. It's Bonnie Clutter's body, in a long-sleeved navy-
     blue dress; but her head is wrapped in layers and layers of
     white cotton gauze, and lacquered with a shiny substance -
     like an enormous cocoon. Truman stares.

                                        CUT TO:

26 **INT. WALKER HOTEL, TRUMAN'S ROOM - NIGHT**   26

     Truman on the PHONE to Jack in Brooklyn. One of Truman's
     trunks is open, displaying bottles of liquor, packaged and
     tinned gourmet food, and stacks of unused yellow legal pads.
     He drinks, standing at the window.

                    JACK (OVER PHONE)
          I think I scared a friend of yours
          this morning. He came looking for
          you while I was writing.

                    TRUMAN (ON PHONE)
          You hate my friends.

                    JACK
          I wouldn't say hate. So long as
          they don't knock on my door.

                    TRUMAN
          I saw the bodies today.

                    JACK
          Which?

                    TRUMAN
          The Clutters. I looked inside the
          coffins.

                    JACK
          That's horrifying.

                    TRUMAN
          It comforts me - something so
          horrifying it's freeing. It's a
          relief. Normal life falls away.
               (beat)
          But, then, I was never much for
          normal life -

                    JACK
          No, you weren't.

                    TRUMAN
          People here won't talk to me. They
          want someone like you, like Nelle.
          Me they hate.

                    JACK
          I can't think of a single quality I
          share with Nelle.

                    TRUMAN
          Well -

                    JACK
          Maybe manliness.

                    TRUMAN
          My point exactly.

                    JACK
          It's why I left the Midwest in the
          first place. I knew I could only
          find someone like you in New York
          City.

On Truman, gazing at the EMPTY TOWN SQUARE below.

                                              CUT TO:

27   **EXT. GARDEN CITY, VARIOUS - EARLY MORNING**   27

A SHOPKEEPER sweeps the sidewalk. There are THANKSGIVING
DECORATIONS in his shop window.

A SCHOOL BUS picks up a SMALL BOY at the intersection of a
DIRT ROAD and the paved COUNTY ROAD.

A SMALL BRIDGE over the Arkansas river. Below them, men are
sifting the riverbed with nets, moving slowly downstream.

                                              CUT TO:

28   **INT. WALKER HOTEL, LOBBY - EARLY MORNING**   28

Nelle waits by the FRONT DESK. The ELEVATOR DOORS open and
Truman emerges. He is DRESSED SOBERLY - NO LONG SCARF, NO
LONG COAT. He walks toward Nelle, then TURNS as if he's a
runway model, walks away, turns again and walks back. He
stops a few feet in front of her. Nelle refuses to smile.

                    NELLE
          Let's go.

                                              CUT TO:

29   **EXT. HOLCOMB TOWN ROAD - EARLY MORNING**   29

Danny Burke walks down the road with a bookbag over his
shoulder. Nelle approaches him, Truman keeps his distance.

                    NELLE
          Danny?
               (Danny stops)
          Would you mind terribly if I walked
          with you for a bit?

He shrugs. They walk together.

                                              CUT TO:

A30   **EXT. LAURA KINNEY HOUSE - AFTERNOON**   A30

Laura opens door to Truman and Nelle.

30   **INT. LAURA KINNEY HOUSE, KITCHEN - AFTERNOON**   30

Nelle and Laura Kinney sit at the table. Truman stands at
the counter.

>   LAURA
>   I thought you were from the FBI
>   with your long coat.

>   TRUMAN
>   Is that so?

>   LAURA
>   That's why I ran off.

>   TRUMAN
>   I've been getting a lot of that
>   lately.

Truman smiles. Laura smiles back, amused, a bit comforted.

>   LAURA
>   It's fine talking to you all.
>   Practically nobody around here
>   wants to talk since what happened.

>   NELLE
>   Folks have been through a rough
>   patch. Including you.
>   (Laura nods)
>   Nancy was your best friend.

>   LAURA
>   She was my best friend.

They're quiet for a few moments.

>   NELLE
>   How has Danny been?

>   LAURA
>   Pretty shattered. Nothing terrible
>   ever happened to him before. Nancy
>   just started wearing his ring again
>   after this huge fight - Mr. Clutter
>   was trying to get her to end it
>   'cause Danny's Catholic.

>   NELLE
>   What were the Clutters?

                        LAURA
          Methodist. Danny was the last
          person at the house that night.
          That's why Mr. Dewey's keeps
          interviewing him - they don't think
          he had anything to do with it -
          just to see if he remembers
          anything unusual and all.

                        NELLE
          People in town seem to wonder if he
          was involved.

                        LAURA
          That's been real hard for Danny.

                        TRUMAN
          Oh, it's the hardest - when people
          have a notion about you and it's
          impossible to convince them
          otherwise.
          Since I was a child folks have
          thought they had me pegged because
          of the way I look and the way I
          talk. They're always wrong.
               (looks at her)
          Do you know what I mean?

Laura stares at him and nods. He's clearly struck a chord.

                        LAURA
          I want to show you something.

She goes in the door to the GROUND FLOOR APARTMENT. They see
her through the LACE CURTAINS getting something from her
DESK, which is stacked with books. Truman whispers to Nelle:

                        TRUMAN
          Not one person here understands
          her.

Laura returns. She hugs a SMALL BOOK to her chest. After a
moment, she holds it out to them.

                        LAURA
          Maybe you'll get a better picture
          of Nancy. And the family.

                        NELLE
          What is this?

                              LAURA
                    It's her diary.

                                                    CUT TO:

31   INT. RENTAL CAR/EXT. NEIGHBORHOOD - AFTERNOON   31

      Nelle and Truman walk quickly back to the hotel. Nelle has
      the diary open.

                              NELLE
                    "Danny here tonight and we watched
                    TV. So nice just having him sit
                    with us. Left at eleven. P.S.-
                    He's the only one I really love."

      She turns the page. The rest of the book is blank.

                              NELLE (cont'd)
                    And that was that.

                              TRUMAN
                    The end of a life.

                                                    CUT TO:

32   INT. WALKER HOTEL, NELLE'S ROOM - LATE NIGHT   32

      Nelle typing. Truman is propped up on pillows on the bed,
      scrunching his eyes to remember what was said that afternoon,
      then writing quickly on one of many YELLOW LEGAL PADS,
      handing the pages of interview dialogue to Nelle. He's
      exhausted. Nelle stops typing a moment, looks through the
      pages Truman has handed her:

                              NELLE
                    "Shattered."

                              TRUMAN
                    "Pretty shattered. Nothing
                    terrible ever happened to him
                    before."

      He pushes some pillows aside and lies down.

                              TRUMAN (cont'd)
                    I have 94 percent recall of all
                    conversations.

                              NELLE
                    94 percent.

                      TRUMAN
          I've tested myself.

                      NELLE
            (scans some of what he's
            written)
          I hate that you're better than me
          at this.

She turns back to the typewriter. She types. Truman lies
there, looking at the ceiling for a few moments. He closes
his eyes. Nelle knows without looking –

                      NELLE (cont'd)
          Don't you dare close your eyes on
          my bed.

No answer. She keeps typing.

                      NELLE (cont'd)
          Stand up and walk out that door.
          Go to your room if you're gonna
          sleep. Truman. Truman.

Nelle turns to look at him. He's asleep. She goes back to
typing. Under her breath:

                      NELLE (cont'd)
          Crap.

                                    FADE OUT.

33   **INT. WALKER HOTEL, BREAKFAST ROOM – LATE MORNING**   33

Truman drinks coffee alone, sleepy. He takes a SMALL BOTTLE
of HOT-PEPPER TABASCO from his jacket pocket and shakes it
over his EGGS. He replaces the bottle in his jacket. Nelle
walks into the lobby from upstairs, heads for Truman.

                      NELLE
          What right do you have being tired?
          You were snoring blissfully –

                      TRUMAN
          I don't snore –

                      NELLE
           – while I lay there, hating you –

                      TRUMAN
          You don't hate me.

                        NELLE
          Not much.
                (She sits. Truman holds
                 out a NOTE)
          What?
                (takes it, looks)
          Marie Dewey?... We've got somewhere
          to go for Thanksgiving supper.

                        TRUMAN
          Apparently Detective Foxy's wife
          has a better opinion of me than
          Detective Foxy.

                                                    CUT TO:

34   **EXT. DEWEY HOME - AFTERNOON**   34

      Ding Dong. We see the FRONT DOOR open. Reveal MARIE DEWEY -
      pretty, 35, dressed primly - and her two boys: ALVIN JR. (9),
      and PAUL (6), lurking behind, curious. Marie smiles.

                        MARIE
          You came.

      Reverse onto Nelle... and Truman, dressed in a DARK SUIT,
      hair neatly combed, like an Exeter schoolboy attending a
      funeral. Nelle smiles.

                        NELLE
          Hi.

      Nelle nudges Truman, who hands over his gifts: a BOTTLE OF
      J&B, and a PACKAGE of GOURMET SPICED NUTS.

                        TRUMAN
                (soberly)
          Thank you for having us.

                        MARIE
                (mock serious)
          Thank *you*.
                (then:)
          Get yourselves in here.
                (turns and walks into the
                 house)
          Alvin! Get your pants on. They're
          here.

      On Nelle and Truman, surprised.

35   **INT. DEWEY HOME, LIVING ROOM - AFTERNOON**   35

A FOOTBALL GAME plays on the television. No one's watching.
We can HEAR Alvin on the phone in his study at the back of
the house.

36   **INT. DEWEY HOME, KITCHEN - CONTINUOUS**   36

Truman and Marie at the stove. Nelle sits at the kitchen
table. Truman has his jacket off and an apron on, as does
Marie. They are peering into a POT OF BLACK-EYED PEAS.
Marie is shaking in drops of HOT PEPPER TABASCO.

>   TRUMAN
>   More. More.

>   MARIE
>   Alvin will hate this.

>   TRUMAN
>   Yes, but we who know the truth will
>   love it.

>   MARIE
>   (laughs)
>   I have to stop.
>   (then)
>   I cannot believe you're from New
>   Orleans. I miss it so much.

>   TRUMAN
>   I only lived there for a short
>   while but my Mama was born and
>   bred.

>   MARIE
>   You know something - Alvin pretends
>   he doesn't know who you are, but
>   the minute you came to town he read
>   your books. He had one of his men
>   pick up "Breakfast at Tiffany's" in
>   Kansas City 'cause it's banned from
>   the library here.

>   TRUMAN
>   What did Mr. Dewey think?

>   MARIE
>   He liked it more than he's willing
>   to admit.

>   TRUMAN
> How very foxy.

Marie smiles at that word used to describe her husband.

>   TRUMAN
> Mama would've put in half the
> bottle by now.

Beat.

>   MARIE
> Alright, one more shake.

37   **INT. DEWEY HOME, HALLWAY - CONTINUOUS**   37

Alvin walks toward the kitchen. He smokes. He looks
exhausted. He hears SQUEALS of laughter.

38   **INT. DEWEY HOME, KITCHEN - CONTINUOUS**   38

Alvin enters. They all stop laughing and look at him. Alvin
nods to Truman and Nelle.

>   TRUMAN   NELLE
> Hello.   Hi.

Silence. Marie sips her drink.

>   MARIE
> How you doing, foxy?

She cracks up.

39   **INT. DEWEY HOME, DINING ROOM - LATER**   39

The remains of dinner. The kids have left. The bottle of
J&B sits on the table, half-empty. Marie's a bit drunk.
Everyone's PLATE is clean except for Alvin's, on which sits a
MOUND of uneaten black-eyed peas. Truman is mid-story.

>   TRUMAN
> I was writing the script as they
> were filming, all that time in
> Italy. I'd work like mad all day
> long and then dash down to the bar
> around midnight to hand in the next
> day's scenes. Humphrey had just
> about moved into the hotel bar-

                    MARIE
               (whispers to Alvin)
          Humphrey *Bogart.*

Alvin knows.

                    TRUMAN
          - where he and John drank every
          night-

                    MARIE
               (to Alvin)
          John *Huston.*

Alvin knows.

                    TRUMAN
          - and I mean drank, like famished
          water buffaloes. Well - I'd only
          just handed them the final scene
          when the bellhop told me I had a
          phone call. It was my stepfather,
          Joe Capote, calling to say that my
          mother had died. I flew home to
          New York - terribly distraught -
          but when I got to the apartment I
          could see that Joe was in even
          worse shape than I was. He grabbed
          my hands and sat me down at the
          kitchen table, and he said to me,
          "Talk. Talk about anything, any
          subject in the world. Don't worry
          whether it will interest me or not.
          Just talk so I won't break down."
          And I did. He couldn't bear to be
          alone with his thoughts. It was
          too painful.

It's quiet for a moment, then Marie looks at Alvin.

                    MARIE
          It's been a hard couple weeks for
          Alvin. He and Herb Clutter were
          good friends. From church.

                    DEWEY
          Marie -

                    MARIE
          Oh come on, Alvin. These are good
          people.

Finally, Dewey looks at Truman and Nelle.

40   INT. DEWEY HOME, STUDY - NIGHT   40

Alvin shows Truman and Nelle the CRIME SCENE PHOTOS from the
Clutter murders. We see the four corpses, BOUND and SHOT,
the bloody footprints in the Clutter basement. Truman and
Nelle stare at the photos of Nancy and Kenyon. Then, quietly-

                    TRUMAN
          Who would put a pillow under the
          boy's head just to shoot him? Why
          would they tuck Nancy in?

                    DEWEY
               (surprised by the insight)
          I want to know the same thing.

Truman hands Nelle one of the photos. She looks at it -

                    NELLE
          Twisted notion of tenderness.

                                              CUT TO:

41   EXT. DEWEY HOME - NIGHT   41

Truman and Nelle are leaving. Alvin and Marie stand in the
front door. Nelle kisses Marie.

                    NELLE
          Thank you.

                    MARIE
          So many of my friends would love to
          meet you.

                    NELLE
          That'd be fine -

                    TRUMAN
               (to Dewey)
          You don't have to worry. I'm not
          going to write about this until
          everything's over.

                    DEWEY
          I'm not worried. I know what room
          you're in at the hotel. And I know
          where you live in Brooklyn.

Truman smiles.

                                              CUT TO:

42   **EXT. GARDEN CITY - VARIOUS - DAY AND NIGHT**   42

MUSIC: "Have yourself a Merry Little Christmas..." Main
Street, CHRISTMAS LIGHTS in the TREES.

The HARDWARE STORE, with Santa Claus DECORATIONS in the
window and a "ONE WEEK LEFT TO BUY YOUR GIFTS..." sign.

                                              CUT TO:

43   **EXT. CLUTTER FARM - LATE AFTERNOON**   43

Truman and Nelle walk with PETE HOLT (70, very frail) on the
Clutter property. Apples rot on the ground, the trees are
bare, signs of disrepair are beginning to weather the house.

                    HOLT
              (re the apples)
          I'd of picked them up but I haven't
          been myself. Mind you, I make the
          walk out here every day, check the
          house, make sure the pipes don't
          freeze - that sort of item. The
          least I can do for Mr. Clutter.

                    NELLE
          How long have you worked here?

                    HOLT
          1940 - a lotta years. The wife
          too, cleaning the house. Cooking.

                    NELLE
          Well, she's marvelous. Lunch was
          wonderful.

                    HOLT
              (ignoring this)
          She had a hard job after what all
          happened. Cleaning. I burned most
          of the rest - mattresses - too far
          of a mess.
              (then, looks at them)
          I've asked around some - if
          anyone's looking for a strong hand.

They don't know what to say. Finally, he looks away.

                    HOLT (cont'd)
          I don't think they'll be able to
          sell the place till they catch the
          ones that did it.
              (MORE)

                    HOLT (cont'd)
              (beat)
          That's what I hear anyhow.

Silence as the three of them look out over the barren fields.

44   **INT. CLUTTER HOUSE, BONNIE'S BEDROOM - DUSK**   44

    Just the bed-frame - the mattress is gone. Truman and Nelle
    find her Bible on the bedside table, her bookmark, see the
    painting of Jesus walking on water. Pete Holt stands off to
    the side, waiting patiently.

                                                        CUT TO:

45   **EXT. WALKER HOTEL LOBBY, GARDEN CITY - NIGHT**   45

    Through the front window we see a Christmas tree in the
    lobby.

46   **INT. WALKER HOTEL, TRUMAN'S ROOM - NIGHT**   46

    Jazzy Christmas music on the RADIO. Nelle sits in the big
    armchair with a drink. She laughs. We HEAR Jack on the phone:

                    JACK (OVER PHONE)
          You're celebrating.

    We see Truman wearing a YELLOW SILK SHORT ROBE with white
    lace, bare legs. He's on the phone and walking, for Nelle's
    enjoyment, back and forth, like a runway model.

                    TRUMAN (ON PHONE)
          Remember Nelle's manuscript she
          sent me in New York?

                    JACK
          Mockingbird. Killing a Mockingbird.
          You said it was good.

                    TRUMAN
          And I was right. She just heard
          Lipincott wants to publish it.

                    JACK (OVER PHONE)
              (pause)
          Well. Jesus. That's terrific.
          Tell her congratulations.

                    TRUMAN
          Congratulations.
               (covers phone, mouths to
               Nelle:)
          Jealous.

                    JACK (OVER PHONE)
          Just promise you'll be home by
          Christmas.

                    TRUMAN
          I can't leave now Jack - I mean it
          was hard at first, but now I'm
          practically the mayor.

He vamps. Nelle laughs.

                    JACK (OVER PHONE)
          Alright.

                    TRUMAN
          I want to come home - I do. Though
          if they catch whoever did this, who
          knows what - I'll probably be here
          til next Christmas.

                    JACK (OVER PHONE)
          Right. I'll let you go.

                    TRUMAN
          Jack, we'll go away this spring to
          write. Maybe Spain...

                    JACK
          Alright, Truman.

                    TRUMAN
          Bye.
               (hangs up)
          The poor boy misses me.

Goes to the mini-bar to fix a drink.

                    NELLE
          Truman.

                    TRUMAN
          Nelle.

                    NELLE
          You remember when we were kids?

                    TRUMAN
          I was never a kid. I was born
          fully formed.

                    NELLE
          I had no idea what a homosexual
          was. But I knew whatever they
          were, you were one of 'em.

Truman puts down his drink and marches out of the room, shuts
the door. Nelle's unsure whether she really insulted him.
From the HALL, we hear a WOMAN SHRIEK, and a MAN saying:

                    MAN IN HALL (O.S.)
          Oh. Uh. Oh. Excuse us.

Truman runs back in, shuts door. They crack up.

                                             CUT TO:

47   **EXT. DEWEY HOME - NIGHT, CHRISTMAS EVE, ESTABLISHING**   47

     Tasteful Christmas lights strung on the BUSHES. A WREATH on
     the FRONT DOOR.

48   **INT. DEWEY HOME, LIVING ROOM - NIGHT**   48

     Truman, Nelle, Marie and Alvin. Drinks. A FULL ASHTRAY on
     the coffee table in front of Alvin. He's distracted,
     smoking. Marie holds a WOMEN'S MAGAZINE, checking what
     Truman says with what's written there.

                    TRUMAN
               (quickly, as if reciting)
          - girdle up - no extra bulges - if
          you're dressed right for him when
          he gets home, the evening should be
          smooth sailing. Bon voyage, gals.

                    MARIE
          I can't believe you got this whole
          page -- I only read it to you once!

          TRUMAN   NELLE
I've trained myself.   ... trained myself.

Truman looks at Nelle.

          TRUMAN   NELLE
I have 94 percent recall.   ... 94 percent recall.

                         TRUMAN
                    (laughing)
              You cut that out.

Alvin stubs out his cigarette - though it still burns. He
stands.

                         MARIE
              You believe that Alvin?

                         ALVIN
              Impressive.

He walks out. Silence.

                         MARIE
              I'm sorry. He's upset.
                    (stubs out cigarette)
              - smoking three packs a day.
                    (then)
              Two men did it. They know who.
              One of them used to have a cellmate
              who gave him up for the thousand
              dollar reward. They passed through
              Kansas City last week writing bad
              checks - by the time Alvin's boys
              got up there they'd skipped out
              again.

                         NELLE
              Where to?

                         MARIE
              They have no idea.

49   **INT. DEWEY HOME, DINING ROOM - LATER**   49

Christmas dinner. Truman, Nelle, Marie and Alvin have just
sat down. They wait for the Dewey boys - Alvin Jr. and Paul.
We hear them in the living room horsing around.

                         DEWEY
              Alvin. Paul. Now.

It's quiet for a second. Then something crashes and breaks.

                         DEWEY (cont'd)
              Damnit.
                    (gets up, goes)
              Come here.

                         MARIE
              Alvin ...

Phone RINGS.

                    DEWEY (O.S.)
          Alvin Jr. Get over here.

                    ALVIN JR. (O.S.)
          Dad, the phone.

                    DEWEY (O.S.)
          Paul. Back to the table.

Dewey returns to the dining room, pushing Paul ahead of him.

                    DEWEY (cont'd)
          Sit.

Alvin Jr. enters.

                    ALVIN JR.
          Dad?

                    MARIE
          Tell them we're at dinner, Alvin.

                    ALVIN JR.
          Dad?

                    DEWEY
          Not now, Alvin.

Alvin Jr. leaves. We hear the PHONE being HUNG UP. Alvin
Jr. returns and sits. They all get ready to say grace, then:

                    ALVIN JR.
          You need to call the Chief of
          Police in Las Vegas when you have a
          minute.

Everyone looks at Dewey.

                                  FADE OUT:

50   **EXT. COURTHOUSE SQUARE, GARDEN CITY - LATE AFTERNOON**   50

OVER BLACK SCREEN we hear the voice of a RADIO ANNOUNCER.

                    RADIO ANNOUNCER (V.O.)
          ... This is KERG radio, Garden
          City. A friendly broadcast from a
          friendly place. Our lead story:

Slowly, the sounds of a CROWD emerge in the background.

FADE UP ON: HIGH SCHOOL kids sitting on the hood and front seat of a CHEVY parked at the edge of a CROWD of 200 people. Truman watches. It is COLD. A fat, shivering CO-ED reads the headline in the Kansas City Star: "Police Fear Lynch Mob." The CAR RADIO is on.

                    RADIO ANNOUNCER (V.O.) (cont'd)
          ... newsmen from six states have
          joined scores of Kansans as they
          await the arrival of confessed
          killers Perry Smith and Richard
          Hickock. KBI officers have been
          driving the Clutter family's brutal
          killers nonstop from...

Truman moves from the car into the large crowd. Old ladies; ranchers; local businessmen; moms with kids; journalists INTERVIEWING citizens; photographers lined up at the bottom of the COURTHOUSE STEPS. We hear snippets of conversation as we pass. A CITIZEN is being interviewed by a JOURNALIST; a MOM WITH BABY standing with a FRIEND; a MIDDLE-AGED man in an overcoat CRYING silently.

Truman approaches Nelle and Marie Dewey, standing together at the curb in front of the courthouse, near the photographers. They are talking quietly, turn to Truman -

                    NELLE
          Hey.

We hear LOUD CROWD NOISE at the south end of the square. A CONVOY of FOUR CARS enters the square. It pulls around to the front of the courthouse. STATE TROOPERS spill out of the lead and rear CARS. Nye gets out of the second car. He opens the back door. The crowd falls SILENT. Two state troopers get DICK HICKOCK - handcuffed, pale - out of the car and lead him up the steps. FLASH. FLASH.

Dewey and Church open the third car's back door. Silence. They retrieve PERRY SMITH. Perry is extremely SHORT, STRONG, ODDLY BEAUTIFUL, with the dark skin and hair of his American Indian mother, and the pug features of his Irish father. As he stands, he has trouble straightening his stubby LEGS, as if they are arthritic. Truman stares.

                    MARIE
               (whispers to Truman)
          Motorcycle accident. He broke them
          and they never healed right.
               (Truman looks at her)
          Alvin told me.

Truman watches Perry, transfixed. Perry seems terrified of the crowd, all the faces, like a child.

Perry scans the crowd. His eyes fall on Truman. FLASH.
FLASH. Truman and Perry look at each other as Perry is led
slowly past. At the top of the steps the COURTHOUSE DOORS
slam shut.

                                                    FADE OUT:

51   **EXT. SHERIFF'S RESIDENCE (4TH FLOOR OF COURTHOUSE) - MORNING** 51

      FADE IN: Truman knocks on the door, a NEWSPAPER, a BOOK, and
      a PAPER BAG in his hand. On the door it says "SHERIFF'S
      RESIDENCE - PRIVATE". Dorothy Sanderson opens the door.

                          DOROTHY
                Truman Capote.

                          TRUMAN
                Dorothy Sanderson. I figured you'd
                be left alone this morning by that
                hard-working husband of yours.
                     (holds up bag)
                So I have breakfast.
                     (holds up paper)
                I have news.
                     (book)
                And I have literature. My friend
                Jack mailed me the book you wanted.

      He presents book. Dorothy, flattered, takes it, reads the
      inscription inside.

                          DOROTHY
                "For the maiden of the Midwest, the
                priestess of the plains, the queen
                of the kitchen: my first novel.
                Truman."

      It is "Other Voices, Other Rooms" and we see on the back of
      it the INFAMOUS JACKET PHOTO of Truman at 23 draped sexily on
      a couch. Truman curtsies. The PHONE RINGS.

                          DOROTHY (cont'd)
                You're too much. Go on into the
                living room, lemme grab that - it's
                been ringing all morning.

52   **INT. SHERIFF'S RESIDENCE, FOYER - CONTINUOUS**   52

      Truman walks into the residence. To the left is the kitchen;
      to the right is the living room. Truman looks back at
      Dorothy - she's still on the phone. He heads for the
      kitchen.

INT. SHERIFF'S RESIDENCE, KITCHEN - CONTINUOUS

Truman walks slowly through the doorway of the large kitchen.
On the far side of the kitchen is a JAIL CELL. Inside the
cell is PERRY SMITH. (Now we know why Truman came here.)

Truman STARES. Perry doesn't see him - he's resting his head
on a small table, the tip of his THUMB in his mouth. The
chair seems too tall for Perry. He looks like a lonely
kindergartner, told to take his afternoon nap. After several
moments, Dorothy enters, flustered:

> DOROTHY
> Oh. Truman. I meant in there.
> (points to living room)
> I... um...

Perry sits up quickly, rubs his legs.

> DOROTHY (cont'd)
> It's the women's cell. It's hardly
> ever used. But they wanted to, um,
> separate... Please. Let's sit in
> the living room. I'll set up in
> the living room.

She gathers a tray of Truman's PASTRIES, and COFFEE CUPS.

> DOROTHY (cont'd)
> Come.

She goes - Truman starts to follow, then lingers.

> TRUMAN
> They put you in the women's cell.

> PERRY
> Among other indignities.

Perry's voice is oddly high, whispery - special words are
precisely enunciated.

> TRUMAN
> Well... she's a good cook.

> PERRY
> She's scared of me.

> TRUMAN
> I think so am I. A little bit.

                              PERRY
                    Are you?
                         (a moment, then:)
                    You have any aspirin? My legs -

          Dorothy's in the doorway.

                              DOROTHY
                    Um. Truman? All set.

          Truman looks at Dorothy, looks back at Perry.

                              TRUMAN
                    I'm sorry.

                                                       CUT TO:

54   INT. COURTROOM - DAY   54

          Judge ROLAND TATE, white-haired, imperious, bangs his gavel.
          The packed crowd quiets down. Perry and Dick sit at the
          defense table chewing JUICY FRUIT GUM. Next to them: their
          aged court-appointed lawyer, Franklin Weeks (70).

          Dick wears a SHIRT AND TIE. Perry wears jeans rolled up at
          the cuff, his SHIRT OPEN at the collar. He draws on a piece
          of paper with a STUBBY PENCIL - a rather good picture of a
          LARGE PARROT. Truman sits with Nelle, watching Perry -

                              TRUMAN
                         (murmurs)
                    His feet don't touch the floor.

                              JUDGE TATE
                    In the matter of the State of
                    Kansas v. Richard Eugene Hickock
                    and Perry Edward Smith this Court
                    has been informed by counsel - Mr.
                    Weeks - that defendants wish to
                    waive their right to Preliminary
                    Hearing. Mr. Hickock, is that your
                    wish?

          Hickock looks at Weeks. Weeks nods. Hickock stands.

                              HICKOCK
                         (unconvincing)
                    Yessir. Yes.

          Hickock sits. Truman whispers to Nelle -

                              TRUMAN
                    Why are they doing that?

                    JUDGE TATE
          Mr. Smith.

                    PERRY
               (stands... then:)
          I ask that the waiver be
          effectuated.

Judge Tate looks at him for a moment -

                    JUDGE TATE
          So noted.
               (bangs gavel)
          We're adjourned.

Crowd gets up. Much talk. Truman watches Perry and Dick
through the forest of bodies. They are led away in
handcuffs. Franklin Weeks stands slowly, then begins
gathering his things - he's old and it takes him ages to
collect his papers. Truman watches.

                                        CUT TO:

55   **EXT. SHERIFF'S RESIDENCE - AFTERNOON**   55

     Truman knocks. He holds a PIE. Dorothy answers.

                    DOROTHY
          Mr. Capote.

                    TRUMAN
               (offers pie)
          Madame Sanderson.

                    DOROTHY
          Is that for the two of us to share?
          Or for me to eat alone while you
          talk to our guest?

Truman is caught. He smiles.

56   **INT. SHERIFF'S RESIDENCE, KITCHEN - AFTERNOON**   56

     Truman sits near the bars of the cell. Perry draws on a
     scrap of paper at the small table. Dorothy watches from the
     door to the living room. The BOOK Truman gave to Dorothy
     lies on the floor next to Perry's meticulously made bed.

                    TRUMAN
          Was it your choice to waive the
          hearing?

Perry doesn't answer. Dorothy checks her watch, leaves.
Truman takes a bottle of BAYER ASPIRIN out of his pocket.

> TRUMAN (cont'd)
> You still need some?
> (Perry doesn't move)
> Give me your hand.

Perry extends his hand through the bars. As Truman shakes
some aspirin into it -

> PERRY
> I could kill you if you got too
> close.

Perry puts the aspirin in his mouth, CHEWS THEM, holds out
his hand for more. Truman gives him more, which Perry puts
in his pocket for later.

> TRUMAN
> Would you like some water?

Perry shakes his head. Silence.

> TRUMAN (cont'd)
> Mrs. Sanderson lent you my book -

> PERRY
> He said we'd curry favor with the
> Judge if we waived our rights.

> TRUMAN
> Who did?

> PERRY
> The lawyer.

> TRUMAN
> Okay.

Truman nods, not wanting to push this any further. Perry
picks up the book, holds it out through the bars.

> PERRY
> Your picture's undignified. People
> recall first impressions.

> TRUMAN
> What's been your first impression?

> PERRY
> You want something.

                    TRUMAN
          From you?

Dorothy pokes her head in from the living room.

                    DOROTHY
          Truman. Walter's gonna be home
          soon.

                    TRUMAN
               (to Perry)
          I just want permission to talk.
               (then)
          Has anyone else visited?

Perry doesn't answer.

                    DOROTHY
          Truman -

                    TRUMAN
          Will you tell me if you need
          anything? I can have whatever you
          want sent from New York.
               (no answer)
          Will you do that?

On Perry, considering whether to trust this man.

                                        CUT TO:

57 **INT. NEW YORKER, WILLIAM SHAWN'S OFFICE - LATE AFTERNOON**   57

Phone RINGS, WILLIAM SHAWN answers (50, New Yorker editor,
conservatively attired) at a desk looking onto 44th Street.

                    SHAWN
          William Shawn.

                    TRUMAN (OVER PHONE)
          Gorgeous?

                    SHAWN
          Truman.

INTERCUT to Truman in a PHONE BOOTH outside the COURTHOUSE.

57A   **INT. COURTHOUSE PHONEBOOTH - DAY**   57A

                  TRUMAN
     I'm writing a book. It's too much
     for a single article - this town,
     the killers most of all - you will
     be stunned by Perry Smith -

                  SHAWN
     Why? What has he -

                  TRUMAN
     Not much yet, but I *know*. I can
     sense him. He's desperately
     lonely, frightened.... I have
     questions - are you ready?

                  SHAWN
     Would it matter -

                  TRUMAN
     How much more money can you send
     me? How quickly can you get Dick
     Avedon out here to take some
     pictures?

INTERCUT to WILLIAM SHAWN'S OFFICE. On Shawn -- he doesn't
know how to begin to respond.

                                    CUT TO:

58   **INT. HICKOCK'S JAIL CELL - DAY**   58

Perry has been placed in an adjoining cell for the afternoon.
He COMBS his greased hair in a mirror. A camera FLASHES.

Nelle and Truman sit outside the cells. Franklin Weeks dozes
off to the side. RICHARD AVEDON - small, dark, wiry,
flamboyant - is snapping photos of a bare-chested Hickock in
the next cell, particularly his TATTOOS, while Hickock
chatters away.

                  HICKOCK
     Perry, honey. You look terrific...

Perry is embarrassed, glances over at Truman. FLASH.

                  HICKOCK (cont'd)
     Calm yourself down, sweetheart.

Perry glances at Nelle. She MOTIONS to him that his SHIRT is
buttoned wrong. Perry fixes it, looks back at her.

Hickock notices Truman gazing at his tattoos - the one on his CHEST: the word PEACE, with a cross radiating rays of light.

> HICKOCK (cont'd)
> Be patient, Capote. Maybe later
> they'll send you my skin.

> TRUMAN
> I have the perfect place for it,
> over the hearth.

Hickock smiles. FLASH. Truman looks over at Perry, sitting alone. Truman starts to remove his TIE.

PHOTOS, in quick succession: Of Hickock pulling up his sleeve to reveal his tattoos. Of Perry combing his HAIR. FLASH. The GRINNING CAT on Hickock's hand. FLASH. Perry looking directly at the camera. FLASH.

                                        CUT TO:

59   **INT. COURTHOUSE - MORNING, ONE MONTH LATER**   59

Series of shots in and around the courthouse:

TITLE UP: "One month later"

An officer approaches down a long hallway. A janitor cleans the basin of the water fountain. Spectators are drawn into the courthouse. The officer opens the courtroom doors. A crescendo of sounds.

60   **INT. COURTROOM - DAY**   60

Spectators take seats. The jury files back into the box. Perry and Dick chew gum. Perry wears TRUMAN'S TIE, and draws on a pad with a NEW SET OF COLORED PENCILS - another PARROT, quite beautiful, now YELLOW. Nelle and Truman sit together.

> NELLE
> Where'd Perry get the art set?

Truman shrugs. Nelle raises her eyebrows. Judge Tate GAVELS loudly, looks to the jury.

> JUDGE TATE
> Members of the jury. Have you
> reached a verdict?

> FOREMAN
> (stands)
> Yes sir.

                    JUDGE TATE
          Defendants rise.

Perry and Dick stand. Judge Tate turns back to the Foreman.

                    JUDGE TATE (cont'd)
          Perry Edward Smith and Richard
          Eugene Hickock stand accused of
          four counts of the crime of murder
          in the first degree. Have you
          reached a unanimous verdict?

                    FOREMAN
          We have, your honor.

                    JUDGE TATE
          What is your verdict?

                    FOREMAN
          Guilty. On all counts.

                    JUDGE TATE
          Have you unanimously reached a
          sentence.

                    FOREMAN
          We have, your honor.

                    JUDGE TATE
          What is the sentence?

                    FOREMAN
          Death.

Judge nods, the foreman sits. Judge turns to Perry and Dick.

                    JUDGE TATE
          Perry Edward Smith and Richard
          Eugene Hickock. You've been found
          guilty of four counts of murder in
          the first degree. You will be
          taken to the state penitentiary at
          Lansing. No later than midnight,
          May 13 of this year, nineteen
          hundred and sixty, each of you will
          be hanged by the neck until dead.
          So ordered.

He GAVELS. Perry and Dick are set upon by Sheriff's Deputies
and led out. Photographers crowd them. Dick turns to Perry.

                    HICKOCK
          Alright, partner. Least now we're
          not the only killers in Kansas.

Perry looks at him, utterly lost. FLASH.

                                                CUT TO:

61   **INT. WALKER HOTEL, NELLE'S ROOM - JUST BEFORE DAWN**   61

Nelle sits at the window, smoking. Truman in the armchair,
holding a drink. They've been up all night. Their bags are
packed. Also - a few packed boxes of written-in yellow
notepads and many typed pages. Truman glances at his watch.

                        TRUMAN
            You think he slept at all?

Nelle looks over at him.

                        TRUMAN (cont'd)
            I need to see him before we go.

                                                CUT TO:

62   **INT. SHERIFF'S RESIDENCE - MORNING**   62

Truman sits next to Perry's cell. Perry lies on the bed,
staring at the ceiling.

                        TRUMAN
            They're going to transfer you up to
            Lansing today. You'll have to make
            sure to put me on the visitor's
            list. Otherwise I can't see you.

No response.

                        TRUMAN (cont'd)
            Will you do that? I'm going to
            help find you a proper lawyer. You
            need a serious lawyer for an
            appeal.
                 (no response)
            They took Dick last night. I need
            you to get him to do the same thing
            - put me on the visitor's list.
            Will you do that, Perry?

Perry closes his eyes.

                        TRUMAN (cont'd)
            Perry.

                                                FADE OUT.

63   **INT. TRUMAN AND JACK'S HOUSE, LIVING ROOM - NIGHT**   63

FADE UP ON the sounds of a HUGE PARTY in progress. We see a
home-made BANNER reading "Return to Civilization!"   The
CAMERA follows NELLE as she walks through the crowd: Gays,
straights, smoke and noise. Society women, slender and
beautiful; BEN BARON pontificating to CHRISTOPHER ISHERWOOD.

                    BEN BARON
          Nelle. Kudos on "Kill the Bird."
          Is that it?

                    NELLE
          Close enough. Thanks.

William Shawn talks to a MUCH TALLER WOMAN.

                    SHAWN
          He hasn't written a word yet,
          though he says it's the nonfiction
          book of the decade...

We HEAR Truman before we see him:

                    TRUMAN (O.S.)
          He's little, but terrifying -

We see Truman in the corner entertaining a small group. Jack
Dunphy stands off to the side. Nelle settles next to Jack.

                    TRUMAN (cont'd)
          He's as short as I am. And almost
          as pretty. I'd be with him right
          now but he's being given new
          accommodations -

Guests laugh.

                    TRUMAN (cont'd)
          Most people assume he's a monster.
          I don't see him that way. The book
          I'm writing will return him to the
          realm of humanity -- it's the book
          I was always meant to write...

Nelle and Jack stand back, watching.

                    JACK
          Watch out. This is the start of a
          great love affair.

                    NELLE
          Oh yes. Truman in love with Truman.

65   **INT. LE PAVILLON RESTAURANT - DAY**   65

Truman is being interviewed over lunch.

> TRUMAN
> ... I was in Marilyn's apartment
> just last week. I had to break it
> to her that, of the four Matisses
> hanging on her wall, two were
> upside down.

The REPORTER laughs. A waiter passes. Truman taps his glass.

> TRUMAN (cont'd)
> Another.
> (to reporter)
> To answer your question, I'm
> following "Breakfast at Tiffany's"
> by blazing a different path - by
> inventing an entirely new kind of
> writing: the non-fiction novel.

> REPORTER
> You have a subject?

Truman takes a last sip of his drink -- utterly serious now.

> TRUMAN
> On the night of November 14, two
> men broke into a quiet farmhouse in
> Kansas and murdered an entire
> family. Why did they do that?
> It's been suggested that this
> subject is tawdry - it's not worthy
> of literature. I disagree. Two
> worlds exist in this country - the
> quiet conservative life, and the
> life of those two men - the
> underbelly, the criminally violent.
> Those worlds converged that bloody
> night. I spent the past three
> months interviewing everyone in
> Kansas touched by that violence. I
> spent hours talking to the killers -
> and I'll spend more.
> (waiter brings his drink)
> Researching this work has changed
> my life, altered my point of view
> about almost everything. I think
> those who read it will be similarly
> affected.
> (he sips)
> (MORE)

                    TRUMAN (cont'd)
          Such a book can only be written by
          a journalist who has mastered the
          techniques of fiction -

                    REPORTER
          You're speaking of yourself.

                    TRUMAN
          You're really very clever.

                                        CUT TO:

66   **INT. TRUMAN AND JACK'S HOUSE, BEDROOM - DAY**   66

     Truman sits in bed, writing on a yellow LEGAL PAD, surrounded
     by PILES of notes. He squints his eyes, concentrating. Jack
     enters, delivers a CUP OF COFFEE. Truman doesn't notice.

67   **INT. TRUMAN AND JACK'S HOUSE, BEDROOM - LATER**   67

     Truman is rifling through the boxes, looking for particular
     notes. He can't find what he needs. The phone RINGS.

                                        CUT TO:

68   **EXT. STREET, BROOKLYN HEIGHTS - LATE AFTERNOON**   68

     Jack and Truman walk.

                    TRUMAN
          Perry's decided to appeal. He
          claims their attorney was
          incompetent - that he never raised
          the issue of temporary insanity.

                    JACK
          So you find them a new lawyer.

                    TRUMAN
          They're facing execution in six
          weeks, Jack. They need someone to
          argue whether or not that's right.

                    JACK
          Okay.

                    TRUMAN
          I'd also like to see them alive,
          yes, thank you very much. I need
          to hear their story.

     They walk in silence for a few moments.

                    TRUMAN (cont'd)
          If you met him you'd understand.
          It's as if no-one's ever asked him
          a single question about himself.
          He's so... damaged - and strange -
          unexplored....
                    (then)
          I don't trust this Hickock fellow.
          Perry's the only person who can
          describe to me what happened that
          night. I need to hear him say it.

                    JACK
          Just be careful what you do to get
          what you want.

                    TRUMAN
          I'm finding them a lawyer.

                    JACK
          Truman. You're finding yourself a
          lawyer.

                                                CUT TO:

69   **INT. CAR, DRIVING, TWO-LANE KANSAS HIGHWAY - DAY**   69

     Truman drives alone, concentrating intently. He has to
     stretch to see over the dashboard.

70   **EXT. KANSAS STATE PENITENTIARY (KSP), LANSING - DAY**   70

     A turreted, Civil War-era fortress an hour's drive from
     Kansas City. Truman pulls up to the GUARDHOUSE.

71   **INT. KSP, WAITING ROOM/WARDEN'S OFFICE - DAY**   71

     Truman waits alone, looking at the lone decoration: a
     campaign poster, showing a fat man in a suit grinning while
     holding a shotgun. Across the bottom it reads: WALK TALL
     WITH KRUTCH. A YOUNG PRISON GUARD sticks his head out of the
     office door.

                    YOUNG PRISON GUARD
          Warden Krutch will see you now.

72   **INT. KSP, WARDEN'S OFFICE - DAY**   72

Wood-paneled walls, government-issue desk. On the wall
behind the desk is a CHART - a racial accounting of the
current inmate population. It reads: WHITE - 1405, COLORED -
360, MEXICANS - 12, INDIANS - 6.

WARDEN MARSHALL KRUTCH is fat, coarse, sweaty even in winter.
And it's spring. He's running for Congress - there are
"KRUTCH FOR CONGRESS" bumper stickers laying around the
office. He's enjoying a chance at a little publicity. The
YOUNG PRISON GUARD stands quietly by the wall.

                    KRUTCH
          We do well by our boys. Showers
          once a week. Feed em good. We'll
          be feeding Perry Smith in the
          infirmary soon if he don't eat.
          Get the food in through his arm.

                    TRUMAN
          What are you talking about?

                    KRUTCH
          Hasn't eaten in a month. But it's
          not his right to kill himself.
          It's the People's right. The
          People of this State. And that's
          who I work for, the People. You
          can write any of this down.

                    TRUMAN
          No one told me.

                    KRUTCH
          Yah. Won't eat.

                    TRUMAN
          When can I see him?

                    KRUTCH
              (checking desk calendar)
          How about you come back Thursday?

                    TRUMAN
          No. That's no good. I need to see
          them now, then whenever I want for
          as long as I want.

                    KRUTCH
          Not how we do things here.

Pause.

                        TRUMAN
         I see.

Truman glances at the campaign stickers, the young prison
guard, then back at Krutch.

                        TRUMAN (cont'd)
         I understand what a burden
         unlimited visitation might be - on
         this institution, and on the People
         who pay for it. I want to be clear
         that I don't expect the citizens of
         Leavenworth County to have to
         shoulder that burden.

Truman reaches into his jacket, pulls from it an ENVELOPE
STUFFED with CASH. He lays it on the desk.

                        TRUMAN (cont'd)
         To be dispensed as you see fit.

Krutch is stone-faced as he regards the money. Finally:

                        KRUTCH
         I didn't know where to count your
         boy - being half-Indian. I did him
         a favor though.
              (points to race chart)
         Counted him White.

                        TRUMAN
         You're a kind and generous man.

                                              CUT TO:

73   **INT. KSP, DEATH ROW - DAY**   73

The second floor of a small building in the corner of the
prison complex. Decrepit. The one hall is lit by mesh-
covered BARE BULBS in the ceiling. Twelve cells - six on
each side. Each is 7 by 10 feet, with one small, high WINDOW
covered by bars and wire. The YOUNG PRISON GUARD opens the
heavy GATE at the end of the hall and shows Truman in.

They walk down the row of cells. In one of them we notice
Lowell Lee Andrews (20, white, spectacled, ENORMOUSLY FAT)
peering at his own face 4 inches from a mirror.

Dick is leaning against the bars of his own cell. He smiles.

                        HICKOCK
         My hero.

                    TRUMAN
          Hello.

                    HICKOCK
          Thanks for your help with the
          lawyer.

                    TRUMAN
          That's fine.

                    HICKOCK
          You must be desperate for a story
          to come all the way out here.

                    YOUNG PRISON GUARD
          Mr. Capote. You're entitled to go
          in. You may, um, go in. If you
          wish.

Truman hesitates for a second.

                    HICKOCK
          You want to see Perry. Go ahead.

                    TRUMAN
          Thank you.

Truman walks to the next cell.

                    HICKOCK
          Ask me, he's just trying to prove
          the insanity defense.

Truman sees Perry, gaunt, lying on his cot, almost comatose.
Perry's rather striking drawing of a LARGE YELLOW PARROT sits
propped on his table. An UNEATEN LUNCH TRAY lies on the
floor - a cockroach runs over it. Truman watches, disturbed.

                                        CUT TO:

74   **INT. SUPERMARKET - NIGHT**   74

     Camera follows Truman as he walks down an aisle with a small
     WICKER BASKET. He stops, looks at a shelf.

75   **INT. SUPERMARKET - NIGHT**   75

     Truman waits in the check-out line behind a MOM paying for
     her groceries.

Her SON (3) stands next to her legs, wearing a little cowboy
hat and cradling a TOY GUN to his chest. He sucks his thumb.
Truman and the boy look at each other.

                                              CUT TO:

76   **INT. KSP, DEATH ROW, PERRY'S CELL - DAY**   76

Truman sits on the chair, his WICKER BASKET on the table. He
has spread out a cloth napkin. A GUARD watches from outside
the cell. Perry lies completely still on the cot. Truman
takes out jars of BONNET BABY FOOD, inspects the labels.

                     TRUMAN
                  (to Perry)
            I don't care what your plans are
            for yourself ...

He decides on the CUSTARD jar. He opens it, takes a plastic
BABY SPOON from the basket.

                     TRUMAN (cont'd)
            But you're gonna wake up enough to
            tell me what you did with my tie.

He spoons a bit into Perry's mouth. The GUARD walks away.
Truman leans close to Perry, whispers:

                     TRUMAN (cont'd)
            It's okay. It's Truman. It's your
            friend.

76A **INT. KSP, DEATH ROW, PERRY'S CELL - LATER (LATE AFTERNOON)** 76A

Perry sleeps. Truman stands against the wall watching him.
He has cleaned up the basket of food. He walks over to
Perry's desk, sees two handwritten notebooks on it: THE
PRIVATE DIARY OF PERRY EDWARD SMITH and PERSONAL DICTIONARY.
Next to them, he sees a pencil SELF-PORTRAIT Perry drew.
It's very good. Truman touches it.

76B **INT. KSP, DEATH ROW, PERRY'S CELL - LATER (EVENING)**   76B

Perry sleeps. Truman sits on the chair watching, waiting.
Perry opens his eyes, looks at Truman.

76C **INT. KSP, DEATH ROW, PERRY'S CELL - LATER (NIGHT)**   76C

Perry is sitting up a bit, Truman helps him sip a cup of
water. Perry lies back down. He's looking at Truman.

                         TRUMAN
          How'd you learn to draw like that?

Perry closes his eyes.

                                                CUT TO:

77   **INT. CAR, DRIVING - AFTERNOON (NEXT DAY)**   77

      Truman drives through the KANSAS STATE PENITENTIARY gate,
      waves to the Guard.

78   **INT. KSP, DEATH ROW, PERRY'S CELL - EVENING**   78

      Perry sits on the bed, cleaned up, wet hair neatly combed,
      looking at a few OLD SNAPSHOTS he has saved in a
      handkerchief. Truman sits in the chair across from him.
      Perry hands him a photo of his mother. Perry speaks quietly.

                         PERRY
          Before she had us. Before she
          started drinking.

                         TRUMAN
          Who took care of you as a child?

                         PERRY
          Orphanage. Me and Linda.

                         TRUMAN
          That's your sister?

Perry nods. Truman waits for more. It doesn't come.

                         TRUMAN (cont'd)
          We're not so different as you might
          think. I was abandoned repeatedly
          as a child. My mama'd drag me
          along to some new town so she could
          take up with another man she'd met.
          Night after night she'd lock me in
          the hotel room - Mama'd turn the
          latch and tell the staff not to let
          me out no matter what. I was
          terrified - I'd scream my head off -
          till finally I'd collapse on the
          carpet next to the door and fall
          asleep. After years of this she
          just left me with relatives in
          Alabama.

                    PERRY
          Who raised you up?

                    TRUMAN
          My Aunts.
               (Perry nods)
          That's when I met Nelle - she lived
          next door.
               (looks again at the photo,
                hands it back)
          Your mother was Indian?

                    PERRY
          Cherokee.

                    TRUMAN
          Drinking was not a good thing for
          her.

                    PERRY
          No tolerance for it.

                    TRUMAN
          And your father?

                    PERRY
          No tolerance for him either.

Truman's laughs, surprised by the joke, though it's unclear
whether Perry meant it as one. He stares at Perry.

                    TRUMAN
          What I can't decide is if you
          understand how fascinating you are.

Perry doesn't respond, then -

                    PERRY
          I'm sorry about your tie. They
          took it away from me because we're
          all on suicide watch. It's why the
          lights stay on at night.

                    TRUMAN
          I hope we're past that now. You
          had me worried.

                    PERRY
          Okay.

                    TRUMAN
          I don't care about the tie. It's
          just a pity because it looked so
          good on you.

Perry leans in, motions toward Dick's cell, lowers his voice -

> PERRY
> Be careful of Ricardo. I think he
> wants you all to himself.

> TRUMAN
> Alright -

> PERRY
> But he's naturally mendacious - not
> to be trusted - if he had a hundred
> dollars he'd steal a stick of
> chewing gum.

> TRUMAN
> You wouldn't.

Perry shakes his head. Then, Truman nods toward Perry's
notebooks.

> TRUMAN (cont'd)
> I want to take your notebooks with
> me - I want to read them.

Perry hesitates.

> TRUMAN (cont'd)
> If I leave here without
> understanding you, the world will
> always see you as a monster. I
> don't want that - I don't see you
> that way.

A moment, then Perry reaches for the NOTEBOOKS, hands them to
Truman. Then he hands Truman the DRAWING he did of himself.

> PERRY
> I tracked my father down in Alaska.
> I was 14. One day I said to him,
> "Mom's dead." I could see it. A
> week later we got the news. She
> finally drunk herself to death.

Truman regards Perry. Then he looks at the drawing -

> TRUMAN
> This is remarkable.

> PERRY
> Sometimes you see a thing - how it
> really is.

On Truman holding the drawing, looking at Perry.

80   **EXT. KANSAS STATE PENITENTIARY PARKING LOT - NIGHT**   80

Truman walks quickly to his car, holding Perry's DRAWING and
NOTEBOOKS. At the car, he looks back at the dark jailhouse.

                                            CUT TO:

81A   **INT. HOTEL ROOM, KANSAS CITY - LATE NIGHT**   81A

Truman at the desk, PERRY'S TWO BOOKS next to a LEGAL PAD
already filled with notes. He's on the PHONE with Nelle,
paging through the PERSONAL DICTIONARY captivated by it.

                    TRUMAN (ON PHONE)
He trusts me - that's why he gave
it to me. He's given me absolutely
everything.
        (paging through Diary)
You should see his drawings, Nelle,
how good he is. He wants so badly
to be taken seriously, to be held
in some esteem.

INTERCUT with Nelle, in pajamas, sitting on the porch of her
home in Monroeville, smoking.

81B   **INT. NELLE'S LIVING ROOM - NIGHT**   81B

                    NELLE
Do you?

                    TRUMAN
Do I what?

                    NELLE
Hold him in esteem?

                    TRUMAN
Well... he's a gold mine. I mean
he's told me his *entire life*, and
now it's all here for me to write
down - All of the history I need.
His *entire life* in this Diary. His
dead mother. A brother and sister
killed themselves.

                    NELLE
You tell him your mama did the same
thing?

                         TRUMAN
          I tell him everything. We've been
          talking our heads off the past
          month. Sometimes, when I think how
          good my book can be, I can hardly
          breathe.

                         NELLE
          Huh.

                         TRUMAN
               (finds what he wants)
          Here's what I wanted to read to
          you:
          "If Called Upon to Make a Speech:" -
          this is exactly what I was talking
          about - a speech just in case he's
          ever recognized for an achievement:
          "If Called Upon to Make a Speech:
          I can't remember what I was going
          to say for the life of me. I don't
          think ever before have so many
          people been so directly responsible
          for my being so very, very glad.
          It's a wonderful moment and a rare
          one. Thank you!"
               (beat)
          There's an exclamation point on the
          end of that thank you, in case you
          didn't catch it...
               (Silence)
          Where'd you go?

     We hear Nelle exhale her cigarette.

                         NELLE
          Christ. I guess it stopped being
          funny.

                         TRUMAN
          I never said it was.
               (turns a page)
          Listen to this...

                                             CUT TO:

81C   **EXT. KANSAS CITYSCAPE - VARIOUS (TWO WEEKS ELAPSE)**   81C

82   **INT. DINER, DOWNTOWN KANSAS CITY - MORNING**   82

     Truman is eating breakfast with Alvin Dewey. A WAITRESS
     refills their coffees.

                    DEWEY
               (to waitress)
          Thanks.

She leaves. An uncomfortable silence. Then:

                    DEWEY (cont'd)
          You're nothing if not hard-working.

                    TRUMAN
          You look good, healthy again.

                    DEWEY
          Not a chance.

Dewey taps a cigarette out of his pack.

                    TRUMAN
          I've decided on a title for my
          book. I think you'll like it -
          very masculine. "In Cold Blood."

                    DEWEY
               (lights the cigarette)
          That refers to the crime or the
          fact that you're still talking to
          the criminals?

                    TRUMAN
          The former, among other things.

                    DEWEY
          I see.

They eat for a moment. Then:

                    TRUMAN
          I've been wanting to ask if you'll
          let me look at your investigation
          notes.

                    DEWEY
          That lawyer you helped find for
          your friends got them a hearing at
          the Kansas Supreme Court -

                    TRUMAN
          I heard this morning.

                    DEWEY
          - on the issue of inadequate
          counsel.

> TRUMAN
> Alvin. Do you not want me to look
> at your notes? You are permitted
> to say no.

> DEWEY
> (rises, takes out wallet)
> I'll tell you what: if those boys
> get off, I'm coming to Brooklyn to
> hunt you down.

Truman can't decide whether Dewey is kidding or not. Dewey
puts money on the table.

> DEWEY (cont'd)
> I have to be in court at nine
> o'clock.

He walks away. Over his shoulder:

> DEWEY (cont'd)
> Call Roy Church. He'll show you
> what you want to see.

CUT TO:

83   **INT. KSP, DEATH ROW - DAY**   83

Truman walks down the hall. He passes Dick's cell. Dick is
lying in bed. Dick rises and smiles widely at Truman.

> HICKOCK
> Hey, hey...

Truman smiles, puts HIS FINGERS TO HIS LIPS, continues past.
He stops outside Perry's cell. Perry (looking MUCH
HEALTHIER) is drawing at his table -- a picture of the HUGE
YELLOW PARROT swooping down from the sky. Truman watches for
a few moments, then Perry looks at him.

84   **INT. KSP, DEATH ROW, PERRY'S CELL - MOMENTS LATER**   84

The Guard locks Truman inside with Perry.

> PERRY
> Thank you.

Truman looks at the Guard - he leaves.

                    TRUMAN
          It was as much for me as for
          anyone. I couldn't bear the
          thought of losing you so soon.

                    PERRY
          We're going to be able to use your
          book for our case. You'll write we
          never got to raise our insanity
          plea. You wrote how terrible the
          lawyer was?

                    TRUMAN
          I haven't written a word yet.

Beat.

                    PERRY
          What have you been doing?

                    TRUMAN
          Research. Waiting to talk to you.

                    PERRY
          All right.

                    TRUMAN
          I had hoped -

                    PERRY
          What are you calling it?

                    TRUMAN
          The book?
              (looks directly at him)
          I have no idea.

Pause.

                    TRUMAN (cont'd)
          If I'm going to write about you -
          if I'm going to determine *how* to
          write about you - you need to tell
          me about that night at the Clutter
          house.

Perry just looks at him.

                    TRUMAN (cont'd)
          Perry.

Perry shakes his head.

                    TRUMAN (cont'd)
          Why? Do you worry what I'll think?

Perry looks away. A long moment.

                    TRUMAN
          Is that it?

Silence. Then:

                    PERRY
          Dick says you know Elizabeth
          Taylor.

                    TRUMAN
          I know a lot of people.

Truman gives up for now. Sees the PICTURE OF THE YELLOW BIRD
on the desk.

                    TRUMAN (cont'd)
          What is that you keep drawing?

                    PERRY
          You must hate having to come to
          this place -

                    TRUMAN
          Perry, I have invitations to be in
          Morocco, Greece.... I choose to be
          here. Those people have
          everything, all their prayers have
          been answered, yet they're more
          desperate than ever. I prefer to
          be here with you.

                    PERRY
               (looks at Truman; evenly)
          I was ten, I wet the bed, the nuns
          at the orphanage hated the smell.
          First month one of them found me
          shivering - just trying to get
          through the night. The Sister
          pulled back the covers and shined
          her flashlight to see what I'd did.
          The sheets were wet. She hit me so
          many times with that flashlight she
          broke it.
               (he shrugs)
                    (MORE)

                    PERRY (cont'd)
          That night I dreamed about the
          yellow bird. Tall. Yellow like
          the sun.
          It picked me up and it clawed the
          Nun's eyes - and it lifted me into
          the sky.

They look at each other.

85 **EXT. BAR, DOWNTOWN K.C. - NIGHT**   85

Truman on the street outside the club at a PAY PHONE. He
talks with Jack in Brooklyn.

                    TRUMAN
          I'm just missing this one piece,
          Jack. Be patient with me.

                    JACK
          How long is that gonna take? Why
          don't you try leaving him alone for
          a while? Come to Spain. You can
          always visit him later.

                    TRUMAN
          I don't know.

                    JACK
          Well, I'm off. I've got my own
          writing to do.

                    TRUMAN
          Do it in Brooklyn. Wait for me.

                    JACK
          Too many people around.
             (beat)
          I'll leave the address on the
          kitchen table. Truman, what do you
          do there when you're not with him? -
          It must be awful.

Truman's watching a YOUNG GUY standing outside the bar,
looking at him.

                    JACK
          Think about what I said. Join me
          when you can.

                    TRUMAN
          I will. I will. Bye.

Truman follows the YOUNG GUY into the bar.

87A   **INT. HOTEL ROOM, KANSAS CITY - LATE NIGHT**   87A

Truman sleeps. He OPENS HIS EYES in bed. Turns to the
bedside table to see the drawing of Perry looking at him.

                                                CUT TO:

87B   **EXT. KANSAS CITY - DAWN**   87B

A young drifter stands alone on an empty street corner. He
checks a pay phone for a coin. It's empty.

                                                CUT TO:

88   **INT. KSP, DEATH ROW, PERRY'S CELL - DAY**   88

Perry is lying on his cot reading an ADVENTURE MAGAZINE -
something to do with finding buried treasure off the coast of
Mexico - and sucking on the tip of his thumb. After a moment
he STARTLES and looks up.

Truman stands outside his cell. He holds a stack of books:
Perry's PERSONAL DICTIONARY and DIARY, and a new WEBSTER'S
DICTIONARY and THESAURUS.

                        PERRY
            I didn't see you. Jesus, you...
                (stands, tucks in shirt)
            Come in. Where's the guard?

                        TRUMAN
            I can't. I brought you some
            things, but I have to fly back
            East.

                        PERRY
            When?

                        TRUMAN
            An hour. I'm sorry.

                        PERRY
            You can't.

                        TRUMAN
            I'm sorry.

                        PERRY
            Who are you going there to see-

                    HICKOCK (O.S.)
                 (from next cell)
            Capote, get it straight in your
            book - we never intended on killing
            that family -

                    PERRY
            I told him that.

                    HICKOCK (O.S.)
            No premeditation -

                    PERRY
            I told him!

Perry searches the cell for something else to give to Truman
to keep him there. Then, he stops. He has nothing left to
give, and is unwilling to talk about that night at the
Clutters. He becomes very still. Truman speaks gently -

                    TRUMAN
            Your writings are magnificent. I
            hope these help you do more.

No response. Truman places the books on the floor just
outside Perry's cell -- Perry's writings in one stack and the
new dictionaries in another right next to it.

                    TRUMAN (cont'd)
            I have so much material - from the
            trial, from our visits, your
            journals. I have to organize it
            all, and I have to start the
            process of writing.
                 (no response)
            I'll visit soon. Perhaps this fall.
                 (backing away)
            I miss you already. Write me every
            five minutes.

He turns and goes. We stay with Perry as Truman leaves. We
hear Dick speak to Truman.

                    HICKOCK (O.S.)
            Be good now.

Hear Truman's footsteps receding. Then, a long shot of the
hallway as the Guard lets Truman out the gate at the end of
the row. Silence.

90A   **INT. KSP, DEATH ROW, PERRY'S CELL**   90A

    Perry looks down at the books sitting on the floor outside
    his cell. He crouches, puts his hand through the bars and
    touches the cover of the new dictionary. He's alone.

                                  FADE OUT.

    Over black - the sound of a JET airplane - loud, then
    passing.

95   **EXT. BEACH - DAY**   95

    FADE IN: BRIGHT WHITE SKY. Sounds of seagulls. Ocean, sand,
    cottage houses in greenery set back from the beach.

96   **EXT. RENTED COTTAGE HOUSE - DAY**   96

    The house Jack rented. Jack types on the upstairs deck.
    Truman pulls up in an OLD TAXI. Jack looks out over the
    railing to the street. Jack emerges on the FRONT PORCH as
    Truman walks up the path with his bags. They look at each
    other. Then Truman looks around at the incredible garden,
    the ocean in the background, and starts to LAUGH.

                                    FADE OUT.

    Title up: "January, 1962"

    Sound of a MANUAL TYPEWRITER over black.

97   **EXT. RENTED COTTAGE HOUSE - EARLY MORNING**   97

    FADE IN on the peaceful outside of the house. Sound of
    TYPING.

98   **INT. RENTED COTTAGE HOUSE - EARLY MORNING**   98

    More typing. A PHONE rings. CAMERA tracks slowly through
    the pretty, tiled living room, toward a DOOR at the far end.

99   **INT. BEDROOM, RENTED COTTAGE HOUSE - EARLY MORNING**   99

    Truman at his DESK, surrounded by piles of filled YELLOW
    PADS, NOTE CARDS, an open TRUNK of random notes. He is at
    the MANUAL TYPEWRITER. The phone is on the floor, ringing.
    He types. The phone rings. Exasperated, he picks up.

TRUMAN (ON PHONE)
What.

SHAWN (OVER PHONE)
Truman. I was supposed to be home
for dinner with my wife three hours
ago - I have not been able to tear
myself away from your book. It's
that good. It's not good, it's
astonishing. This first half is
astonishing. If the second half
lives up to this it - it - how much
is left to do?

INTERCUT with Shawn's OFFICE at the New Yorker, NIGHT. Shawn
has a stack of manuscript pages on his desk.

100A **INT. NEW YORKER, WILLIAM SHAWN'S OFFICE**   100A

TRUMAN
I'm already well into the third
part, but I - I can't finish that
till I convince Perry to describe
the night of the killings to me. I
was planning to visit this fall,
see -

SHAWN
I think you need to talk to him
now.

TRUMAN
And we all need to see how this
ends for the final part. I can't
finish the book till I know what
happens. If Perry and Dick are
executed it's one thing - and if
not, well -

SHAWN
Truman. You got your ending -

TRUMAN
I really don't know -

SHAWN
The Kansas court denied their
appeal. It came over the wire on
Friday. You need to talk to Perry
now. He'll be dead by September.
I'm sorry, I know how much you've
come to care about him.

Truman is completely immobile.

                    SHAWN
          Truman?

                    TRUMAN
          Right. Yes. Right.

                    SHAWN
          I want to set up a reading for you
          in the fall, in New York. We'll
          build some interest, and we'll
          publish in the fall.

On Truman.

                                        CUT TO:

101   **INT. KITCHEN, RENTED COTTAGE HOUSE - MORNING**   101

          Truman at the stove watching his tea water heat up. Jack
          enters with a HUGE BASKET of WINE and GROCERIES.

                    TRUMAN
          Plums. Thank god. We have nothing
          in the house.

He takes one from the basket. Jack starts to unpack food.

                    TRUMAN (cont'd)
          Why aren't you working?

                    JACK
          I knew you couldn't be depended on
          to stock the kitchen.

Truman looks at him blankly.

                    JACK (cont'd)
          What would we feed our famous
          guest?

                    TRUMAN
          Oh, Jesus. I completely forgot.

He helps Jack put away the groceries. Then:

                    JACK
                 (utterly nonchalant)
          Plus -- I finished my novel
          yesterday.

Truman looks at Jack, smiles widely.

                                              CUT TO:

102   **EXT. BEACH - NIGHT**   102

Truman, Jack and Nelle. A BONFIRE, a wind-up Victrola
playing Ella Fitzgerald, bottles of wine. Jack and Nelle
dance. Truman toasts Jack drunkenly.

                    TRUMAN
          My man, my hero, my talented... My
          man...

                    JACK
          You said that.

                    TRUMAN
          You are the hardest worker, the
          most unsung talent I know. As
          Nelle passes by on her way to
          London to sell her book which needs
          no selling, may a little of her
          success rub off on both of us.

Jack laughs.

                    JACK
          Here, here!

Nelle tries to smack Truman but can't catch him. The song
changes to a slow one. Jack and Truman dance sweetly
together. Nelle sits on the sand and watches.

                                              CUT TO:

103   **EXT. UPSTAIRS DECK, RENTED COTTAGE HOUSE - MORNING**   103

Breakfast. Truman and Nelle are sitting - Nelle has a small
envelope in her hand. Truman is obviously uncomfortable. As
Jack delivers a platter of omelettes to the table:

                    NELLE
               (to Truman)
          When was the last time you wrote
          back to him?

                    TRUMAN
          I don't know.

                    JACK
          What's this?

                              NELLE
                    A letter for your boyfriend I was
                    asked to deliver.

                              TRUMAN
                    From Perry.

                              JACK
                    Let's have it.

Jack sits. Nelle opens the letter, reads:

                              NELLE
                    "Dear Friend Truman. Where are
                    you? Read this item in a medical
                    dictionary: "Death by hanging is
                    caused by asphyxia, by fracture of
                    the cervical vertebrae, by
                    laceration of the trachea." Not
                    too comforting as we lost our
                    appeal. Missing you - alone and
                    desirous of your presence. Your
                    amigo, Perry."

Pause.

                              TRUMAN
                    Mr. Shawn told me about the court
                    decision yesterday.

                              JACK
                    I was wondering why you were in
                    such a good mood. Surely, I
                    thought, it's not because I
                    finished my little book.

                              TRUMAN
                    That's a terrible thing to say.

Jack looks out at the ocean.

                              TRUMAN (cont'd)
                         (to no one in particular)
                    I used to write him all the time.
                    I've been so focused lately on the
                    book.

                                             CUT TO:

104   **EXT. RENTED COTTAGE HOUSE - DAY**   104

Truman and Nelle carry her bags down the front walk toward a
waiting TAXI.

                    TRUMAN
          Jack says I'm using Perry, but he
          also thinks I fell in love with him
          when I was in Kansas. How both of
          those things can be true is beyond
          me.

                    NELLE
          Did you? Fall in love with him.

Silence as they load the bags into the trunk.

                    NELLE (cont'd)
          Truman? –

                    TRUMAN
          I don't know how to answer that....
          It's as if Perry and I started life
          in the same house. One day he
          stood up and walked out the back
          door while I walked out the front.
          With some different choices, he's
          the man I might have become.

                    NELLE
          Are you kidding me?

Truman shrugs, doesn't answer. Nelle kisses him.

                    NELLE (cont'd)
          Be nice to Jack. Sometimes I think
          he's what I like about you best.

                    TRUMAN
             (smiles)
          I'll see you at the reading in New
          York.

                    NELLE
          The sixteenth.

Nelle gets in the taxi, then leans her head out the window.

                    NELLE (cont'd)
          Truman. Honestly. Are you going
          back to Kansas because you care
          about Perry or because you need
          information before he's killed?

                    TRUMAN
          Can't it be both?

                    NELLE
          No. I don't think it can be.

She drives away. Truman watches her go. He turns back up toward the house, stops a moment to pick a FLOWER from the bushes at the front gate.

                                                    CUT TO:

105   INT. KSP, DEATH ROW - DAY   105

A Guard walks down the corridor carrying a SINGLE FLOWER. He delivers it to Perry, then walks off. Perry is confused. He hears FOOTSTEPS approaching, but can't see who it is.

                     HICKOCK (O.S.)
            Hey, buddy. Thanks.

More footsteps. CAMERA on Perry as the footsteps finally arrive outside his cell. He's shocked.

REVERSE onto Truman, looking tanned, healthy, very blond. He holds a STACK OF BOOKS with a BOW on top. He smiles.

                                                    CUT TO:

106   INT. KSP, DEATH ROW - LATER THAT NIGHT   106

LONG SHOT of dimly lit corridor, light spilling out from each cell. A ROW GUARD walks the hall. We hear voices murmuring.

SIX MORE GUARDS arrive at the top of the stairs. The ROW GUARD walks over, unlocks the GATE to let them in.

107   INT. KSP, DEATH ROW, PERRY'S CELL - NIGHT   107

Perry is looking at the cover of a BOOK - "WALDEN POND." Other books sit next to Perry on the cot. Among them - WILLA CATHER's "MY ANTONIA", also "GREAT EXPECTATIONS" -

                     PERRY
            What was he in jail for?

                     TRUMAN
            They said it was not paying his
            taxes. But really for being an
            outsider - refusing to go along.

Perry nods, looks at the other books.

                     TRUMAN (cont'd)
            You don't have to read any of these
            if you don't want to.
                     (MORE)

> TRUMAN (cont'd)
> But I thought you'd like something
> decent. You're much too smart for
> adventure magazines.

Through the bars of Perry's cell, we can see the SIX GUARDS
enter Lowell Lee Andrew's cell (diagonally across the
corridor). The ROW GUARD appears at Perry's cell.

> ROW GUARD
> Lock-down while Lowell goes to
> solitary. Nobody in or out.
> (to Truman)
> You want in or out?

Truman looks at Perry, then back to the Guard.

> TRUMAN
> In.

108 **INT. KSP, DEATH ROW, LOWELL LEE ANDREW'S CELL - MOMENTS**   108
LATER

The SIX GUARDS start to pack up Andrews cell while he sits on
the cot and watches.

109 **INT. KSP, DEATH ROW, PERRY'S CELL - LATER**   109

Perry and Truman talk very QUIETLY. (Throughout this scene,
we see in the background, across the corridor, the mostly
obscured cell of Andrews. We see his incredibly FAT LEG
being shackled, his belongings being packed in boxes.)

> PERRY
> Everyone says he's a genius. I
> don't think he's a genius. He's
> rich and he went to college - like
> any of us would've if we got the
> chance. He came home for Christmas
> and shot his parents -

> TRUMAN
> - in front of the television.

> PERRY
> You remember the story -

> TRUMAN
> They were watching Father Knows
> Best.

They look at each other and smile. Then:

                    PERRY
          I won't be sorry to see him go.
          Always correcting my grammar.

They watch Andrews being shackled in the background.

                    PERRY (cont'd)
          Now - Dick and me - we're next in
          line.

Truman regards Perry, who looks down.

                    TRUMAN
          I'm so sorry I've been away.

                    PERRY
          It was a long time.

                    TRUMAN
          I know.

                    PERRY
          I wish you could come next week,
          when they take him out to the
          Corner, but the whole prison shuts
          down.

                    TRUMAN
          I have to be in New York anyway.

Perry nods.

                    PERRY
          How's the book going?

                    TRUMAN
          Very slowly.

                    PERRY
          Will you show it to me?

                    TRUMAN
          I've hardly written anything.

One of the six guards CLANGS Andrews' cell bars with his
stick.

                    GUARD #1
          Ready.

The ROW GUARD opens the cell door. Andrews is led out, arms
and legs shackled, into the corridor.

                    HICKOCK
          Keep your head high, buddy.

                    ANDREWS
          Alright now.

                    HICKOCK
          ... or they won't be able to rope
          you under your fat fucking chin.

Andrews is led past Perry's cell. He looks in at Perry.

                    ANDREWS
          Next!

Andrews shuffles down the hall. Perry watches him go. On
Truman watching Perry. We hear the GATE slam shut.

                                        CUT TO:

111   **INT. THEATER - EVENING**   111

Packed. Nelle stands with William Shawn, who receives well-
wishers. BEN BARON enters, seeing Nelle.

                    BEN BARON
               (loudly, over the hubbub)
          Hello Hollywood. That's quite a
          bundle you sold your book for.

Nelle is embarrassed, mostly for Baron, to have the issue of
money brought up publicly.

                    NELLE
          Well...

Baron moves past, Nelle smiles politely, whispers to Shawn.

                    NELLE (cont'd)
          What a gentleman.

112   **INT. THEATER, BACKSTAGE ROOM - MOMENTS LATER**   112

Truman sits alone. In the background, we can HEAR the noise
of the huge crowd gathering in the theater. Truman wears his
MOST STYLISH LITERARY OUTFIT: a gorgeous dark green Knize
SUIT over a black cashmere turtleneck sweater, and horn-
rimmed GLASSES (which we've never seen him wear before).

He's frozen with anticipation, nervousness. After several
moments a THEATER ASSISTANT opens the door.

> YOUNG ASSISTANT
> Mr. Capote. Can I get you
> anything?

> TRUMAN
> No.
> (clears his throat)
> Thank you.

The assistant leaves. We hear the crowd quiet down. Truman
rises slowly, walks through the door to the backstage area.
We hear William Shawn on stage.

> SHAWN (O.S.)
> Welcome New Yorkers...

112A **INT. WINGS/STAGE - NIGHT**   112A

Shawn pauses briefly for a laugh that doesn't come. Truman
continues walking toward the backstage curtains.

> SHAWN (O.S.)
> Thank you for coming to the first
> public reading, the first offering
> of any kind, of Truman Capote's new
> work "In Cold Blood." Our magazine-

Truman walks on stage. Loud applause. Shawn sees him,
slinks back to his seat. Truman walks over to the podium,
takes in the enormous crowd. Once it is completely quiet:

> TRUMAN
> Hello. My name is Truman Capote.

People laugh and applaud loudly.

CUT TO:

113 **INT. KSP, DEATH ROW, PERRY'S CELL - SAME TIME, NIGHT**   113

Perry, eating dinner alone at his table, looks up. We HEAR a
LOUD ENGINE revving outside.

115 **EXT. KSP, THE CORNER WAREHOUSE - SAME TIME**   115

A FRONT-LOADER TRACTOR drives into the warehouse. A PRISON
POLICE CAR parks outside the warehouse.

Guards get the enormous Lowell Lee Andrews, shackled, from the back seat, walk him inside.

116   **INT. KSP, DEATH ROW, PERRY'S CELL - NIGHT**   116

C/U on Perry, now standing on his chair and watching out the tiny window.

                                                    CUT TO:

117   **INT. THEATER, NYC - NIGHT**   117

Truman on stage reading.

                    TRUMAN
          Perry Smith's voice was both gentle
          and prim - a voice that, though
          soft, manufactured each sound
          exactly - ejected it like a smoke
          ring issuing from a parson's mouth.

                                                    CUT TO:

119   **INT. KSP, DEATH ROW, PERRY'S CELL - SAME TIME**   119

Perry watches through his window. From inside the warehouse we hear the gallows TRAP DOOR spring and CLATTER. On Perry,

                                                    CUT TO:

119A   **INT. THEATER, NYC - SAME TIME**   119A

Truman reading. Utter silence except for his voice.

                    TRUMAN (V.O.)
          The village of Holcomb stands on
          the high wheat plains of western
          Kansas, a lonesome area that other
          Kansans call "out there." Until
          one morning in mid-November 1959,
          few Americans - in fact, few
          Kansans - had ever heard of
          Holcomb. Like the waters of the
          [Arkansas] river, like the
          motorists on the highway...
          exceptional happenings had never
          stopped there.

120   **EXT. KSP, DEATH ROW BUILDING - SAME TIME**   120

    We see the outside wall with Perry and Dick's faces peering
    out through their tiny windows.

120A   **EXT. KSP, THE CORNER WAREHOUSE - NIGHT**   120A

    The TRACTOR emerges through the warehouse doors. It carries
    in its FRONT SHOVEL the enormous, dead BODY of ANDREWS
    covered by a BLACK CLOTH.

121A   **INT. THEATER, NYC - SAME TIME**   121A

    Truman reading. The audience completely still.

> TRUMAN
> The four coffins, which quite
> filled the small, flower-crowded
> parlor, were to be sealed at the
> funeral services - very
> understandably, for the effect...
> was disquieting. Nancy wore her
> dress of cherry-red velvet, her
> brother a bright plaid shirt; the
> parents were more sedately attired,
> Mr. Clutter in navy-blue flannel,
> his wife in navy-blue crepe; and -
> and it was this especially that
> lent the scene an awful aura - the
> head of each was completely encased
> in cotton, a swollen cocoon twice
> the size of an ordinary blown-up
> balloon, and the cotton, because it
> had been sprayed with a glossy
> substance, twinkled like Christmas-
> tree snow.

                                                CUT TO:

121B   **EXT. KSP, THE CORNER WAREHOUSE - NIGHT**   121B

    The TRACTOR rolls the body into the BED of a waiting PICK-UP
    TRUCK.

121C   **EXT. KSP, DEATH ROW BUILDING - SAME TIME**   121C

    Perry watches through his window.

122   **INT. THEATER, NYC - SAME TIME**   122

Truman reading. The audience transfixed.

> TRUMAN
> Imagination, of course, can open
> any door - turn the key and let
> terror walk right in. [One]
> Tuesday, at dawn, a carload of...
> strangers, ignorant of the local
> disaster - were startled by what
> they saw as they crossed the
> prairies and passed through
> Holcomb: windows ablaze, almost
> every window in almost every house,
> and, in the brightly lit rooms,
> fully clothed people, even entire
> families, who had sat the whole
> night wide awake, watchful,
> listening. Of what were they
> frightened? "It might happen
> again."

He closes his manuscript. Several moments of SILENCE, then
thunderous APPLAUSE.

                                                    CUT TO:

123   **INT. THEATER, BACKSTAGE ROOM - NIGHT**   123

Truman's dressing room. Packed with well-wishers drinking
from bottles of CHAMPAGNE, smoking, toasting, shouting to be
heard. Truman in the corner with Christopher Isherwood, BEN
BARON others, laughing. A LITERARY ENTHUSIAST approaches,
leans in.

> LITERARY ENTHUSIAST
> Your portrait of those men was
> terrifying. Terrifying.

> TRUMAN
> Thank you.

Truman and Isherwood watch him walk away.

> ISHERWOOD
> Your hairpiece is terrifying.

> TRUMAN
> I was going to say the same thing!

Truman laughs loudly. We SEE Nelle look over from across the
room at her friend having the time of his life.

CUT TO:

124   **INT. NEW YORKER, WILLIAM SHAWN'S OFFICE - NEXT DAY**   124

Truman is hung over but immensely gratified. He's with
Shawn.

                    SHAWN
          Everyone was there.

                    TRUMAN
          Tennessee loved it.

                    SHAWN
          Of course he did.

                    TRUMAN
          Should we do more? I was
          terrified, but -

                    SHAWN
          No, Now we get to withhold while
          everyone else talks. Let them do
          the work.

Truman is barely able to suppress his excitement.

                    SHAWN (cont'd)
          This book is going to change
          everything. It'll change how
          people see you as a writer. It'll
          change how people write. You'll
          finish by October?

                    TRUMAN
          I think so. You know they're
          scheduled for next month?

                    SHAWN
          Hanging. Yes. I'll commit as many
          issues as it takes to publish.
          Three. As many as it takes.

                    TRUMAN
          I'm flying to Kansas tomorrow.
          I'll get Perry to talk -

                    SHAWN
          Honestly, what's he got to lose?

Truman smiles at the joke, then stops himself.

>   TRUMAN
>   It really is too awful.
>   Institutionalized sadism.

Shawn nods.

>   SHAWN
>   You'll be able to finish now.

>   TRUMAN
>   As strange as it may sound to you,
>   I'm going to miss him.

>   FADE OUT.

Over black - the sound of a JET airplane - loud, then
passing.

125   **INT. KSP, DEATH ROW, PERRY'S CELL - DAY**   125

Truman, flushed, out of breath, stands outside Perry's cell.
He's just arrived. He holds a FOLDED-UP NEWSPAPER. Perry
sits at his table reading LEGAL DOCUMENTS.

>   TRUMAN
>   When did you hear?

Perry looks up, mistaking Truman's state for shared
enthusiasm. He smiles widely.

>   PERRY
>   Two days ago.

The Guard opens the cell for Truman. Perry holds up one of
the DOCUMENTS.

>   PERRY (cont'd)
>   It's what we've been waiting for.
>   A stay of execution to make a
>   federal appeal.

Truman enters. Perry goes to him and hugs him tightly.

>   PERRY (cont'd)
>   All thanks to you.

On Truman, shocked, being hugged.

>   CUT TO:

126   **INT. KSP, DEATH ROW, PERRY'S CELL - LATER**   126

Truman sits on the bed, his coat still on, watching Perry -
hyped up, talking, walking around the cell.

> PERRY
> Kansas's had it in for me for ten
> years -- in prison the first time,
> at that trial, here. They can't
> corner me now. Not till the U.S.
> Government says so -

> TRUMAN
> Perry, sit down. For a minute.
>   (Perry sits)
> I need you to talk to me...

> PERRY
> We've got all the time in the world
> to talk. About everything. I've
> been thinking about Ricardo. You
> need to stop sending him those
> trashy books. I won't even mention
> the pornography.
>   (getting up)
> I realize he might have trouble
> grasping the literature you gave
> me, but those books only exacerbate
> the problem -- only 'heighten' or
> 'intensify' it. Maybe we should
> start him on a program...

> TRUMAN
> Perry.

> PERRY
> Give him the simple novels first --

> TRUMAN
> Perry.

Perry stops.

> TRUMAN (cont'd)
> I know what exacerbate means.

> PERRY
> Okay. I thought in case...

> TRUMAN
> There is not a word, or a sentence,
> or a concept, that you can
> illuminate for me.
>   (MORE)

                    TRUMAN (cont'd)
          There is one singular reason that I
          keep coming here -

                    PERRY
          Truman -

                    TRUMAN
          ... November 14th, 1959. Three
          years ago. Three years. That's
          all I want to hear from you.

Pause.

                    PERRY
          I've asked you not to --

                    TRUMAN
             (stands up)
          This is ridiculous.
             (to the Guard)
          I'm ready.
             (to Perry)
          I have a plane to catch.
          I found your sister in Tacoma.
          Maybe she'll talk to me about
          something useful.

                    PERRY
          Don't go out there.

The Guard lets Truman out of the cell.

                    PERRY (cont'd)
          Please don't go out there.

The Guard shuts the door.

                    TRUMAN
          This is my work, Perry. I'm
          working. When you want to tell me
          what I need to hear, you let me
          know.

He walks off down the hall. The GATE slams shut.

                                        CUT TO:

127   **INT. PERRY'S SISTER'S HOUSE, KITCHEN - DAY**   127

Cheaply built ranch house. LINDA MURCHAK (30) walks in the
kitchen back door, shuts it.

                    MRS. MURCHAK
          They'll play outside a while
          longer.

Mrs. Murchak looks like a female Perry, dark and small,
attractive and nervous. Through the window, we see THREE
LITTLE CHILDREN playing on a DECREPIT JUNGLE GYM in the yard.
Truman sits at the table, leafing through a PHOTO ALBUM.

                    MRS. MURCHAK (cont'd)
          I don't want them to see that.

                    TRUMAN
          They've never seen these pictures?

                    MRS. MURCHAK
               (shakes her head)
          Too many questions.

She joins Truman again at the table.

We see an OLD PHOTO of the SMITH FAMILY - Linda at age 8,
Perry (5); their older sister, June; their brother Frank;

and the parents: Florence (American Indian) and John (Irish) -
in front of their rundown truck on a desolate road.

                    MRS. MURCHAK (cont'd)
          June's dead. Frank shot himself.
          Now Perry's did what he did. I
          suppose I'm next. Some ruination
          will visit me.

                    TRUMAN
          I don't think life works that way.

                    MRS. MURCHAK
          It does in this family.

Truman turns the page. A PICTURE of Perry (3) and Linda (6),
HOLDING HANDS and splashing in a big mud-puddle in the rain.
Linda is smiling at Perry, who is naked, laughing.

                    MRS. MURCHAK (cont'd)
          I used to love him. He was my
          little doll.

He turns the page. A PICTURE of Perry (6) and Linda (9),
sitting on the back steps of a shack, poking with a stick at
something in the dirt. After a moment, she gets up, clears
coffee cups.

                    MRS. MURCHAK (cont'd)
          He scares me now.

                    TRUMAN
          When was the last time you saw him?

                    MRS. MURCHAK
          Ten years.

She picks up the album to put it away.

                    TRUMAN
          Do you think I could borrow one of
          those pictures?

                    MRS. MURCHAK
               (hands it to him)
          Take the whole thing. I don't
          want'em anymore.
               (then)
          Just... Perry doesn't know where I
          live. He thinks we're still in
          Portland. Please don't tell him
          we're not.

                    TRUMAN
               (he already has)
          Alright.

                    MRS. MURCHAK
          Don't be taken in by my brother.
          He's got this sensitive side he'll
          show. You believe he's gentle, so
          easily hurt. But he'd just as soon
          kill you as shake your hand. I
          believe that.

                                        CUT TO:

128   **INT. KSP, DEATH ROW - NEXT DAY**   128

     Truman slows for a moment as he passes Hickock's cell.

                    TRUMAN
          Hello handsome.

     Hickock just stares at him. Truman, unnerved, moves on to
     Perry's cell.

129   **INT. KSP, DEATH ROW, PERRY'S CELL - CONTINUOUS**   129

     Perry doing pushups. He sees Truman and stops. He stands.
     The Row Guard approaches.

                         ROW GUARD
                  You want to go in?

Truman regards Perry for a few moments, then:

                         TRUMAN
                  Yes.

The Guard unlocks the door. Perry STARTS TO MOVE toward it.
The Guard SLAMS it shut.

                         PERRY
                  What's the name of your book?

No response. Perry can barely control his anger.

                         PERRY (cont'd)
                  What's the name of your book?

                         TRUMAN
                  I don't...

                         PERRY
                  What's the name of your book?

                         TRUMAN
                  I don't know what you're talking
                  about.

Perry picks up a cut-out ARTICLE from the NY Times from his
desk. He reads.

                         PERRY
                  "Truman Capote read last night
                  before a packed audience from his
                  non-fiction book IN COLD BLOOD."

He looks at Truman.

                         PERRY (cont'd)
                  More?
                      (reads)
                  "The true-crime novel tells of
                  killers Richard Hickock and Perry
                  Smith, who brutally murdered a
                  Kansas family three years ago."

                         TRUMAN
                  Who sent that to you?

Perry doesn't answer.

                         TRUMAN (cont'd)
                  Who sent that to you?

                    PERRY
          That's not your goddamn business.

                    TRUMAN
          It is my business, because it's not
          true. The organizers of the
          reading needed a title. They
          picked one - a sensational one, I
          admit - to attract a crowd.

                    PERRY
          They picked it.

                    TRUMAN
          Yes.

                    PERRY
          That's not your title.

                    TRUMAN
          I haven't chosen one yet.

Perry stares at him, not believing.

                    TRUMAN (cont'd)
          How could I choose -

                    PERRY
          You pretend to be my friend...

                    TRUMAN
          How could I choose a title when you
          still haven't told me what happened
          that night? How could I? I
          couldn't possibly.

Long pause. Truman reaches in his breast pocket and extracts
a PHOTO (the one of Perry and Linda splashing in the puddle.)

                    TRUMAN (cont'd)
          I have something from your sister.

He hands it through the bars to Perry. Perry takes it.

                    TRUMAN (cont'd)
          She misses you.

Perry looks at the photo. After a few moments, Truman turns
to the Guard.

                    TRUMAN (cont'd)
          It's alright. I'll go in.

The Guard unlocks the cell. Truman enters. The Guard locks up, walks away. Perry is still looking at the PHOTO.

> TRUMAN (cont'd)
> I'm sorry. I should have told you
> what they made me call the book.
> (touches Perry's arm)
> I couldn't pretend to be your
> friend. The truth is, I can't help
> wanting to be.
> (silence, then:)
> You don't have to tell me anything
> if you don't want to.

Perry looks at the photo of himself and his sister for a long time.

> PERRY
> Look at my belly.

Perry sits on the bed. Then, almost to himself:

> PERRY (cont'd)
> There must be something wrong with
> us. To do what we did.

Truman waits him out, sitting on the chair. Finally, Perry looks at him. When Perry speaks, it is quietly, completely matter-of-fact.

> PERRY (CONT'D)
> We heard there was ten thousand
> dollars in that house. Once we'd
> tied up everybody and searched all
> over, I knew the guy who told us
> about it was wrong. There wasn't
> any money. But Dick wouldn't
> believe it. He went tearing
> through the house again, banging on
> the walls, looking for a safe. He
> said when he was done, he was going
> to come up to Nancy's room and have
> his way with her. I wouldn't allow
> it. I told him that. I sat with
> Nancy.

CUT TO:

130   **INT. CLUTTER HOUSE, NANCY'S ROOM - FLASHBACK, NIGHT**   130

Perry and Nancy. Perry sits quietly on the edge of Nancy's bed. A SMALL BEDSIDE LAMP softly illuminates a portion of the room. We hear Dick banging around downstairs.

STILLS

Clifton Collins Jr. as Perry Smith and Philip Seymour Hoffman as Truman Capote, in the jail cell in Garden City, Kansas, re-creating a photo shoot by Richard Avedon.

Philip Seymour Hoffman as Truman Capote.

Catherine Keener as Nelle Harper Lee, talking with Truman Capote from her home in Monroeville, Alabama.

Chris Cooper as Kansas Bureau of Investigations agent Alvin Dewey.

Truman Capote (Philip Seymour Hoffman) converses with partygoers at a New York City apartment.

Truman Capote (Philip Seymour Hoffman), next to his rental car, looks at the Clutter Farm from a country road in Holcomb, Kansas.

Truman Capote (Philip Seymour Hoffman) and Nelle Harper Lee (Catherine Keener) climb the courthouse steps in Garden City, Kansas.

Alvin Dewey (Chris Cooper) and Perry Smith (Clifton Collins Jr). arrive in a police car at the Courthouse Square for the arraignment.

Truman Capote (Philip Seymour Hoffman) and Nelle Harper Lee (Catherine
Keener) listen to the arraignment procedures in the courtroom.

Perry Smith (Clifton Collins Jr.) stands during the arraignment in the courtroom,
with Dick Hickock (Mark Pellegrino) sitting in the background.

William Shawn (Bob Balaban) at the welcome-home party at Truman and Jack's house in Brooklyn, New York.

Truman Capote (Philip Seymour Hoffman) and Jack Dunphy (Bruce Greenwood) take a walk in a Brooklyn Heights park.

Truman Capote (Philip Seymour Hoffman) makes a grand entrance at the film premiere of *To Kill a Mockingbird* in New York City.

Truman Capote (Philip Seymour Hoffman) speaks to Nelle Harper Lee (Catherine Keener) during the after-party at Sardi's restaurant in New York City.

Perry Smith (Clifton Collins Jr.) and Dick Hickock (Mark Pellegrino) see Capote one last time in a holding cell in the Kansas City Penitentiary on their execution day.

Screenwriter Dan Futterman and director Bennett Miller during filming.

> PERRY (V.O.)
> It was nice in there.

The scene is almost sweet, until we see that Nancy's legs and hands are TIED and her mouth is TAPED.

                                                        CUT TO:

131   INT. KSP, DEATH ROW, PERRY'S CELL - NIGHT   131

   Perry talking to Truman.

> PERRY
> Dick came to get me and we turned
> out the lights and went down to the
> basement, where we had Mr. Clutter
> and the boy. Dick kept saying "No
> witnesses." I figured if I just
> waited him out he'd give up and
> leave them tied up there. We'd
> drive all night, they'd never find
> us. Mr. Clutter's wrists were tied
> to a pipe over his head. He looked
> like he was hurt, so I cut him
> down.

                                                        CUT TO:

132   INT. CLUTTER HOUSE, BASEMENT - FLASHBACK, NIGHT   132

   HERBERT CLUTTER is bound and taped, his hands tied to a PIPE
   on the LOW CEILING. Perry CUTS the rope with a HUNTING
   KNIFE, catches hold of Herb Clutter, lowers him onto a
   mattress box on the floor.

                                                        CUT TO:

133   INT. KSP, DEATH ROW, PERRY'S CELL - NIGHT   133

   Perry talking to Truman.

> PERRY
> We put a box there on the floor so
> he'd be more comfortable.

> PERRY
> He asked if his wife and daughter
> were alright and I said they were
> fine, they were ready to go to
> sleep.
>   (MORE)

                              PERRY (cont'd)
                    I told him it wasn't long till
                    morning when somebody would find
                    them.
                         (beat)
                    He was looking at me. Just...
                    looking at me. Looking at my eyes.
                    Like he expects me to kill him –
                    expects me to be the kind of person
                    who would kill him. I was thinking
                    – this nice man, he's scared of me.
                    I was ashamed. I mean, I thought
                    he was a kind man, a good.... a
                    gentleman. I thought so right up
                    to the moment I cut his throat. I
                    didn't realize what I'd did till I
                    heard the sound.

                                                        CUT TO:

134   **INT. CLUTTER HOUSE, BASEMENT - FLASHBACK, NIGHT**   134

        Herb Clutter gurgling on the floor.

                              PERRY (V.O.)
                    Like some one drowning under water.

                                                        CUT TO:

135   **INT. KSP, DEATH ROW, PERRY'S CELL - NIGHT**   135

        Perry and Truman. Silence, then:

                              PERRY
                    I was staring at him, bleeding on
                    the floor. I told Dick to finish
                    him off, but he wouldn't do it. We
                    couldn't leave Mr. Clutter like
                    that, so I got the shotgun.

                                                        CUT TO:

136   **INT. CLUTTER HOUSE, BASEMENT - FLASHBACK, NIGHT**   136

        Perry approaches with a SHOTGUN. He aims and SHOOTS him in
        the face.

137   **INT. CLUTTER HOUSE, ANOTHER PART OF THE BASEMENT - FLASHBACK** 137
       NIGHT

       KENYON CLUTTER (15) is bound and gagged on an old sofa, a
       pillow under his head. A flashlight illuminates his face. A
       shotgun enters frame, FIRES. An enormous BURST of LIGHT.

138   **INT. CLUTTER HOUSE, HERB AND BONNIE'S ROOM - FLASHBACK, NIGHT** 38

       Bonnie Clutter (40's, small and thin) tied up on her bed.
       Moonlight through the window.

                        PERRY (V.O.)
            We went to Mrs. Clutter's room.

       The DOOR opens. Perry and Dick walk in with a flashlight.
       Perry points the shotgun at Bonnie's face, FIRES. A BURST of
       LIGHT.

139   **INT. CLUTTER HOUSE, NANCY'S ROOM - FLASHBACK, NIGHT**   139

       Perry and Dick enter Nancy's room, shine the flashlight on
       her face. She looks at Perry. She has been crying. After a
       moment, she TURNS HER FACE to the wall, as if she knows what
       is coming and doesn't want to watch it. Perry AIMS the
       shotgun at the back of her head. The FLASHLIGHT switches
       OFF. The shotgun FIRES. A BURST of LIGHT.

                                      CUT TO:

140   **INT. KSP, DEATH ROW, PERRY'S CELL - NIGHT**   140

       Perry and Truman. Perry still on the bed. Truman sits, not
       moving, on the chair. Silence.

                        PERRY
            Then we drove off.

       Silence. Perry looks at Truman.

                    PERRY (cont'd)
            What do you think of me now?

       No answer. Then:

                     TRUMAN
            Added up, how much money did you
            get from the Clutters?

       Perry thinks.

                              PERRY
                 Between forty and fifty dollars.

Truman nods. They sit there for a long time.

                                                      FADE OUT:

141   **INT. HOTEL ROOM, KANSAS CITY - DAWN, CONTINUOUS**   141

       FADE IN: Hands typing on a MANUAL TYPEWRITER.

       Truman typing at the desk. He stops, removes the page from
       the typewriter, places it on top of a SMALL STACK OF PAGES.
       He sits back.

                                                        CUT TO:

142   **INT. PLANE - DAY**   142

       Truman in his seat, sips a drink. He looks out the window.

                                                        CUT TO:

143   **EXT. STREET, BROOKLYN HEIGHTS - LATE AFTERNOON**   143

       Truman walks with his TRAVEL BAG on his shoulder. He takes
       out his KEYS and turns up the steps to his house.

144   **INT. TRUMAN AND JACK'S HOUSE, FRONT HALL - CONTINUOUS** 144

       Truman opens the door.

                              TRUMAN
                 Jack.

       No answer. He walks down the hall to the BEDROOM.

145   **INT. TRUMAN AND JACK'S HOUSE, BEDROOM - CONTINUOUS**   145

       Truman enters, drops his travel bag on the bed, zips it open,
       removes a SMALL STACK OF TYPED PAGES. He walks to his desk.

       On the desk, we see a HUGE STACK OF TYPED PAGES with a title
       page on top which reads: IN COLD BLOOD. Truman lifts the
       HUGE STACK, places the SMALL STACK under it. He smooths out
       the pages, then steps back from it. He calls out:

                              TRUMAN
                 Jack.

No answer. On Truman, standing in the middle of his room.
He has finished all that he can finish, and is lost as to
what to do next.

                                        FADE OUT.

TITLE UP: "One Year Later"

OVER BLACK WE HEAR THE FOLLOWING DIALOGUE COME UP SLOWLY:

                    TRUMAN (V.O.) (cont'd)
          ... I want to give it to you. The
          truth is, I'm desperate to be done
          with it....

FADE IN:

146   **INT. TRUMAN AND JACK'S HOUSE, KITCHEN - DAY**   146

Truman on the PHONE, in pajamas, looking in the FRIDGE.

                    TRUMAN (ON PHONE)
          Mr. Shawn, I.... I've spent four
          years of my life on this book....
          They got a stay of execution
          yesterday.... Another, yes....

He gets out a jar of BONNET BABY FOOD CUSTARD and starts to
eat it. Truman finds a bottle of J&B on the counter and
pours a shot in his custard.

                    TRUMAN (ON PHONE) (cont'd)
          Supreme Court....

He stirs the custard, eats it.

                    TRUMAN (ON PHONE) (cont'd)
          ... It's harrowing - all I want is
          to write the ending and there's no
          fucking end in sight.... No. No,
          I haven't been drinking again....

147   **INT. TRUMAN AND JACK'S HOUSE, BEDROOM - LATER**   147

Truman sits on the bed with a glass of bourbon, staring at
the television. An empty jar of BABY CUSTARD sits on the
bedside table.

148   **INT. TRUMAN AND JACK'S HOUSE, BEDROOM - LATER**   148

Truman on the bed, the television still on, another drink.
We hear a DOORBELL. We hear Jack walk down the hall, answer
the door, shut the door. Jack enters with a TELEGRAM.

                    JACK
        I don't know how you can eat that.
        Perhaps if you weren't drinking so
        much you wouldn't have to.

No response. Jack turns down the television, opens the
telegram.

                  JACK (cont'd)
          (reads)
        "Dear friend Truman. Haven't heard
        from you in such a long while.
        Please help find new lawyer. If
        not, Dick will have to write
        Supreme Court brief himself. Our
        last appeal. What a pair of
        wretched creatures. Please help.
        Your amigo? Perry."

Pause. Jack looks at Truman.

                  JACK (cont'd)
        Your amigo.

Truman stares back. Finally, he turns back to the television.

                  TRUMAN
        Put it with the others.

Jack goes to the DESK and places the telegram on top of a
LARGE PILE OF TELEGRAMS, all from Perry - all, we should
assume, unanswered.

Jack walks out. Truman sips his drink.

149   **INT. TRUMAN AND JACK'S HOUSE, BEDROOM - LATER, EARLY EVENING**149

Truman at the desk, still in PAJAMAS, typing. Jack enters
wearing a TUXEDO, reads over Truman's shoulder. We see:

"...unable to find lawyer despite extensive search. So sorry.
All best, Truman."

                  JACK
        You tried?

Truman extracts the page from the typewriter, folds it, and puts it in an envelope. He takes a sip of his BOURBON.

> JACK (cont'd)
> (walking out)
> You need to get ready.

                                        CUT TO:

150   INT. LIMOUSINE, MOVING - NIGHT   150

Truman and Jack are driven. Both wear TUXEDOS and OVERCOATS. Truman drinks.

151   INT. LIMOUSINE, MOVING - NIGHT, LATER   151

Driving. Truman and Jack sit in silence, then:

> JACK
> At least pretend for Nelle that
> you're having a good time tonight.

The limo turns a corner and we see an ENORMOUS CROWD in front of a THEATER. On the marquee it says: "Opening tonight - TO KILL A MOCKINGBIRD"

It is COLD. Truman and Jack's limo pulls up. An USHER opens their DOOR.

152   EXT. MOVIE THEATER - MOMENTS LATER   152

Truman, obviously drunk, preens and poses on the red carpet for the CAMERAS. Jack watches from the side.

                                        CUT TO:

153   INT. SARDI'S RESTAURANT, OPENING PARTY - NIGHT   153

Huge party in progress. Nelle walks through the crowd. People turn to her saying: "Congratulations"; "Wonderful". She finds Truman sitting at the BAR, receiving a new drink.

> TRUMAN
> Nelle.

She looks UNCOMFORTABLY DOLLED UP for the premiere of her movie.

> NELLE
> I thought I'd find you here.

                    TRUMAN
                (to the bartender)
          Please, another.

He hands Nelle his drink, receives another. After a moment:

                    NELLE
          How are you?

                    TRUMAN
          Terrible.

Beat.

                    NELLE
          I'm sorry to hear that.

                    TRUMAN
          Well. It's torture. Torture...
                (he drinks)
          ... what they're doing to me.

                    NELLE
          Uh-huh.

                    TRUMAN
          Now the Supreme Court. Can you
          believe it? If they win this
          appeal I will have a complete
          nervous breakdown. I may never
          recover. Just pray things turn my
          way.

                    NELLE
          It must be hard.

                    TRUMAN
          It's torture. They're torturing
          me.

                    NELLE
          I see.

Nelle regards him for a moment.

                    NELLE (cont'd)
          And how'd you like the movie,
          Truman?

She puts her drink down on the bar and walks away. Truman
turns back to the bartender, shrugs.

                  TRUMAN
        I frankly don't know what the fuss
        is about.

On Truman, alone at the bar.

                           FADE OUT.

154 **EXT. STREET, OUTSIDE TRUMAN AND JACK'S HOUSE - EARLY MORNING**154

    FADE UP on a PAPER BOY riding his BIKE down the street. New
    buds are on the trees. It is SPRING. The BOY wears a NEW
    YORK TIMES bag slung over his chest and is tossing copies of
    the paper. One of them lands on Truman and Jack's stoop.

155 **INT. TRUMAN AND JACK'S HOUSE, BEDROOM - MORNING**   155

    Phone RINGING. Truman asleep.

156 **INT. TRUMAN AND JACK'S HOUSE, JACK'S TINY OFFICE - SAME TIME**156

    Jack is writing, longhand, at his desk. PHONE is ringing.
    Jack notices that his door is slightly ajar. He kicks it
    shut. The ringing is much quieter. He keeps writing.

157 **INT. TRUMAN AND JACK'S HOUSE, BEDROOM - SAME TIME**   157

    Truman asleep. PHONE ringing. He wakes up, groggy, answers.

                  TRUMAN
        Hello.

                  OPERATOR (OVER PHONE)
        Mr. Capote?

                  TRUMAN
        Yes?

                  OPERATOR (OVER PHONE)
        I have a call from Mr. Perry Smith
        in the Kansas Correctional System.
        Will you accept charges?

Pause.

                  OPERATOR (cont'd)
        Mr. Truman Capote?

                  TRUMAN
        Yes.

                    OPERATOR (OVER PHONE)
          Will you accept charges?

                    TRUMAN
          Oh.
               (no way out of this)
          Uh... Yes.

                    OPERATOR (OVER PHONE)
          You'll accept charges?

                    TRUMAN
          Yes.

                    OPERATOR (OVER PHONE)
          Mr. Smith, you're on the line.

Now Truman's awake. We hear a series of CLICKS, then:

                    PERRY (OVER PHONE)
          Hello.

Truman can't bring himself to speak.

                    PERRY (cont'd)
          Hello? I can't -
               (to someone)
          This doesn't seem -
               (we hear Perry clicking
                the cradle, then:)
          Operator, I don't think you put me -

                    TRUMAN
          I'm here.

Beat.

                    PERRY (OVER PHONE)
          Truman.

                    TRUMAN
          Hello, Perry.

                    PERRY (OVER PHONE)
          They let me make a couple phone
          calls before I go down to
          Holding... You heard the Supreme
          Court rejected the appeal.

                    TRUMAN
          I didn't... I hadn't heard that.

                    PERRY
          Yeah.

Pause.

>   TRUMAN
>   I'm sorry.

>   PERRY
>   Yeah. They let me make two phone
>   calls.

Truman doesn't know what to say.

>   PERRY (cont'd)
>   We've got a date set for the
>   Warehouse, Dick and me. Two weeks
>   and... Finito. April 14.

Beat.

>   PERRY (cont'd)
>   Will you visit me? Truman. Will
>   you come visit?

>   TRUMAN
>   I don't know if I can. I'll try.
>   (beat)
>   I don't know if I can.

We hear over the line a GUARD in the background:

>   GUARD IN BACKGROUND (OVER PHONE)
>   Time, Smith. Hang it up.

>   PERRY (OVER PHONE)
>   Please visit me, Truman. Just...

>   GUARD IN BACKGROUND (OVER PHONE)
>   Time. Smith.

CLICK. Truman sits very still, the phone in his hand.

>   CUT TO:

158   **INT. KSP, DEATH ROW - ONE WEEK LATER, NIGHT**   158

Perry and Dick being shackled, their belongings packed into
boxes. One of the GUARDS in Perry's cell CLANGS the bars
with his STICK.

>   GUARD
>   Ready.

>   CUT TO:

159   INT. KSP, CONFINEMENT CELL - ONE WEEK LATER, NIGHT   159

     Perry lies alone on his cot. The DOOR opens, KRUTCH enters
     with a GUARD.

                         KRUTCH
                    Perry.

     Perry sits up. Krutch sits on the one chair. The Guard
     stands by the door, takes out a PAD and STUBBY PENCIL.

                         KRUTCH (cont'd)
                    You're allowed three names of
                    people you'd like to witness
                    tomorrow. If there's anybody you
                    want, tell me now.

                         PERRY
                    Truman Capote.

     Krutch nods to the Guard who writes the name down. Krutch
     waits, then:

                         KRUTCH
                    Anybody else?

     Perry SHAKES HIS HEAD.

                                                        CUT TO:

160   INT. TRUMAN AND JACK'S HOUSE, BEDROOM - LATE NIGHT   160

     In a chair near the window, Truman sits awake in his pajamas,
     unable to sleep, completely unable to decide what to do. He
     watches Jack sleep. A long time - then Truman walks to the
     closet, gets out a travel bag, starts to pack.

                                                        CUT TO:

161   EXT. IDLEWILD AIRPORT, NEW YORK - DAY   161

     A PLANE takes off.

162   INT. PLANE, FIRST CLASS SECTION - DAY   162

     Truman sits next to William Shawn, who looks exhausted. The
     STEWARDESS is approaching with the DRINKS CART. She collects
     an empty BABY CUSTARD JAR from Truman's tray.

                    SHAWN
          You want anything?

Truman shakes his head.

                                              CUT TO:

163   **EXT. KANSAS STATE PENITENTIARY - DUSK**   163

       OUTSIDE LIGHTS switch on as it gets dark.

164   **INT. KSP, CONFINEMENT CELL - NIGHT**   164

       Perry sits alone. The door opens and a Guard brings in his
       LAST MEAL: three hot dogs, french fries, an ice cream sundae,
       a strawberry soda. The Guard sets it down on the chair.

                         PERRY
               Thank you.
                    (then)
               You sent the telegram to his hotel?

                         GUARD
               Hours ago.

       Perry looks at the CLOCK on the wall: it's after 8pm.

                         PERRY
               May I make a phone call?

                                              CUT TO:

165   **INT. HOTEL ROOM, MUEHLEBACH HOTEL, KANSAS CITY - NIGHT**   165

       PHONE ringing. The CLOCK reads 8:55pm. Empty drinks
       glasses, a custard jar. Truman lies curled in a fetal
       position on the BED. Shawn walks the floor, exasperated.

                         SHAWN
               That's him again.

       Truman is immobile. Phone still rings.

                         SHAWN (cont'd)
               We've never even met. It is
               utterly inappropriate for me to be
               talking to him.

       Shawn gives up, PICKS UP the phone.

> SHAWN (cont'd)
> Yes.... I'm sorry, he's out, gone
> out.... I'm not sure when....

                                                          CUT TO:

166   **INT. KSP, HALLWAY - NIGHT**   166

   Krutch walks with a TELEGRAM PAGE in hand. A Guard follows.
   They pass a WALL CLOCK: 9:40pm.

167   **INT. KSP, CONFINEMENT CELL - NIGHT**   167

   Krutch and Guard enter Perry's cell. Perry hasn't touched
   his meal.

> KRUTCH
> You got a telex.

   Perry nods. Krutch reads:

> KRUTCH (cont'd)
> "Perry. Unable to visit today
> because not permitted. Always your
> friend, Truman."
> (apologetically)
> That's it.

> PERRY
> It's not true, is it?

   Krutch hesitates a moment, then SHAKES his head.

                                                          CUT TO:

169   **INT. NELLE'S KITCHEN, MONROEVILLE - MINUTES LATER**   169

   Nelle on the PHONE looking at a TELEGRAM. The kitchen CLOCK
   reads 10:20pm. She waits a moment till the line is answered.

> NELLE (ON PHONE)
> Mr. Shawn? It's Nelle.... I just
> got this telegram, has he seen it?

   INTERCUT with William Shawn on the phone in Truman's hotel
   room. A TELEGRAM lies on the DESK. Truman lies on the bed.

169A   **INT. MUEHLEBACH HOTEL ROOM, KANSAS CITY - NIGHT**   169A

                    SHAWN (ON PHONE)
        He won't look at it.

                    NELLE
        Would you put him on please?

                    SHAWN
        He won't talk.

                    NELLE
          (calmly)
        Mr. Shawn, if you have to hold him
        down and put the phone on his ear,
        I need to speak to him.

Shawn, terrifically uncomfortable, walks over to Truman and
holds the phone out to him.

                    SHAWN
        It's Nelle.

A moment, then Truman takes the phone. On Truman's face. We
hear, through the receiver, Nelle:

                    NELLE (OVER PHONE)
        Truman.

Truman finally breathes out.

                              CUT TO:

170   **INT. KSP, HOLDING CELL - SAME TIME**   170

Perry is led, SHACKLED, into a holding cell on the ground
floor of the Death Row Building. Dick is already there,
seated, shackled. We HEAR PERRY'S VOICE:

                    PERRY (V.O.)
        "Miss Nelle Harper Lee and Truman
        Capote: Sorry that Truman was
        unable to make it here at the
        prison for a brief word prior to
        necktie party....

The CLOCK reads 11:05pm. Through the WINDOW, we see activity
in the Gallows Warehouse across the yard.

> PERRY (V.O.) (cont'd)
> ... Whatever his reason for not
> showing up, I want him to know that
> I cannot condemn him for it and
> understand....

Perry makes eye contact with the Guard, who CHEWS GUM. The
Guard checks through the SMALL WINDOW in the door, then
approaches Perry, places a STICK OF GUM in Perry's mouth.
Perry CHEWS.

> PERRY (V.O.) (cont'd)
> ... Not much time left but want you
> both to know that I've been
> sincerely grateful for your
> friendship through the years and
> everything else....

CUT TO:

171A   **INT. MUEHLEBACH HOTEL ROOM, KANSAS CITY - NIGHT**   171A

Truman opens the door to the other part of the suite, where
William Shawn is waiting. Truman is fully dressed and ready.
Perry's VOICE:

> PERRY (V.O.)
> ... I'm not very good at these
> things....

173   **EXT. KANSAS STATE PENITENTIARY - NIGHT**   173

TAXICAB pulls up to the prison gates. Perry's VOICE:

> PERRY (V.O.)
> I have become extremely
> affectionate toward you both. But,
> harness time. Adios amigos. Your
> friend, Perry."

174   **INT. KSP, WAITING ROOM OUTSIDE CELLS - NIGHT**   174

Clock reads 11:35pm. Truman sits with Shawn. Truman is
looking at the TELEGRAM from Perry. He folds it, puts it in
the breast pocket of his jacket. Krutch approaches.

> KRUTCH
> I didn't think I'd be seeing you
> again.
> (then)
> You can visit for a few minutes.

Truman stands, turns to Shawn, still seated.

                    SHAWN
     No.

                   TRUMAN
     Come with me.

                    SHAWN
     Truman. No.

Truman goes alone.

175   **INT. KSP, HOLDING CELL - NIGHT**   175

    Perry, Dick, a Guard. Krutch lets Truman in.

                   KRUTCH
     Five minutes.

He exits, closes the door. Truman doesn't know what to say.

                 HICKOCK
       (without rancor)
     He returns. Long time.

                   TRUMAN
     I don't know what you must think of
     me.

                 HICKOCK
     You haven't been foremost on my
     mind lately. As you can imagine.

Dick looks at Perry and smiles. Perry chews his gum and
smiles back, then looks to Truman who seems upset.

                   PERRY
     You got the letter?

                   TRUMAN
     Yes.

                   PERRY
     It's true. I mean I understand why
     you didn't want to come. I
     wouldn't be here either if I didn't
     have to.

                 HICKOCK
     You got that right.

Silence.

          PERRY
You know Ricardo donated his eyes
to science? Next week, some blind
man will be seeing what Dick used
to see.

          HICKOCK
    (laughs)
He'd be better off the way he was.
What I've seen hasn't been so nice
to look at - but I guess it's
better than nothing.
    (he shrugs, to Truman)
They came around with a form.
    (beat)
Hey. You'll be walking down the
street one day in Denver, wherever -
and suddenly these eyes will be
staring at you. Wouldn't that be
something?

          TRUMAN
    (quietly)
It would be.

Krutch opens the door.

          KRUTCH
  Time.

Truman looks at the clock: 11:50pm. Truman turns to Perry
and Dick. Perry stands.

          PERRY
You'll be watching?

          TRUMAN
I don't know. Do you want me to?

          PERRY
I'd like to have a friend there.

          TRUMAN
Okay. Then I will.

Truman looks down, starts to cry.

          PERRY
It's alright.

          TRUMAN
I did everything I could.

                        PERRY
        Okay.

                        TRUMAN
        I truly did.

                        PERRY
        I know.

Truman nods, wipes his eyes.

                        TRUMAN
        Goodbye, Perry.

                        PERRY
        You're not rid of me yet. I'll see
        you in a few minutes.

Truman goes. On Perry watching him leave.

                                        CUT TO:

176   **INT. CORNER WAREHOUSE - NIGHT**   176

    Huge. Dirt floor. Wooden gallows. TWENTY MEN stand around,
    some smoking. Some are silent. Some whisper quietly.

    Journalists. Also, Alvin Dewey and the KBI men: Church and
    Nye. Krutch in front of the gallows with a CHAPLAIN. At the
    foot of the gallows steps, the EXECUTIONER - thin, older, a
    too-large pin-striped suit and stained cowboy hat. Truman.
    William Shawn.

    HEADLIGHTS, then a PRISON CAR enters, stops. Dick is
    extracted from the back seat. He stands, looks at the CROWD,
    then at the GALLOWS. The Guards nudge him forward.

177   **INT. KSP, HOLDING CELL - A FEW MINUTES LATER**   177

    CLOCK reads 12:05pm. Perry sits alone looking at his hands.
    We HEAR A TRAP DOOR SPRING and CLATTER. Perry looks up.

178   **INT. PRISON CAR - NIGHT**   178

    Light rain outside. Perry in the back seat being driven
    across the yard. He looks out his window, sees a PICKUP
    TRUCK drive out of the Corner Warehouse. On it: a BODY
    covered by a BLACK CLOTH.

179   **INT. CORNER WAREHOUSE - NIGHT**   179

The PRISON CAR enters, stops. Perry is removed from the back
seat. He stands, looks at the assembled men, looks at
Truman. He's nudged forward. As he passes DEWEY, he extends
his hand:

>   PERRY
>   Nice to see you.

Dewey is caught off-guard so shakes his hand. Perry is led
to the base of the gallows.

>   KRUTCH
>   Perry Edward Smith.
>   (reads)
>   "For the crime of murder in the
>   first degree, by order of the Court
>   of Finney County and the Supreme
>   Court of the sovereign State of
>   Kansas, you are sentenced to hang
>   until you die."
>   (then)
>   You can say something if you want.

>   PERRY
>   (quietly, to Krutch)
>   Is there anybody from the family
>   here?

>   KRUTCH
>   No.

Perry is disappointed by this information.

>   PERRY
>   Well. Tell them...
>   (he look out at everyone)
>   I can't remember what I was going
>   to say for the life of me...

He stops. Several moments.

Krutch can't tell if he's done. Finally, Krutch nods to the
Guard. Perry is led up the STEPS. The Chaplain follows.

>   CHAPLAIN
>   Though I walk through the valley of
>   the shadow of death, I will fear no
>   evil, for thou art with me.

The Executioner puts the NOOSE around Perry's neck. Perry
chews his gum. Executioner opens a BLACK CLOTH SACK.

Perry looks at the Chaplain reading prayers, looks at the crowd, at Truman.

> CHAPLAIN (cont'd)
> Thy rod and thy staff, they comfort
> me.

The BLACK SACK goes over Perry's head. Truman watches. He stands next to Alvin Dewey.

> CHAPLAIN (cont'd)
> Thou preparest a table before me in
> the presence of mine enemies. Thou
> annointest my head with oil.

The Executioner pulls the handle, Perry drops.

> CHAPLAIN (cont'd)
> My cup runneth over.

On Truman. Then a WIDE SHOT of the inside of the Warehouse: twenty men watching Perry Smith hang, the Chaplain reading.

FADE OUT.

OVER BLACK:

The SOUND of a TELEPHONE RINGING, as heard through the receiver. We HEAR the CLICK of the phone being PICKED UP, then, after a moment, a VOICE:

> NELLE (OVER PHONE)
> Hello.

FADE UP:

180 **INT. HOTEL ROOM, KANSAS CITY - EARLY MORNING** 180

Truman sits on the edge of the bed in his WET OVERCOAT, as if he'd walked in the rain.

> TRUMAN
> Someday I'll tell you about it.
> For the moment, I'm too shattered.

Pause.

> NELLE (OVER PHONE)
> They're dead, Truman. You're
> alive.

> TRUMAN
> It was a terrible experience and I
> will never get over it.
> (MORE)

                    TRUMAN (cont'd)
          (then)
     There wasn't anything I could have
     done to save them.

We hear Nelle light a cigarette.

                    NELLE (OVER PHONE)
     Maybe not.

We hear her exhale slowly.

                    NELLE (cont'd)
     But the fact is, you didn't want
     to.

On Truman,

                                        FADE OUT.

FADE IN: BRIGHT WHITE. AIRPLANE NOISE. COLORS RESOLVE
INTO:

181   **INT. FIRST CLASS SECTION, AIRPLANE - DAY**   181

     Truman, seated on the aisle, next to William Shawn. After a
     long silence, he extracts from his leather briefcase a
     PACKAGE wrapped in BROWN PAPER. Hands it to Truman.

                    SHAWN (cont'd)
     It came to the hotel this morning.
     I told them I'd give it to you.

     The package says KANSAS STATE PENITENTIARY and is addressed
     to Truman. Truman opens it.

     He takes out PERRY'S NOTEBOOKS - the DIARY and PERSONAL
     DICTIONARY. He opens the Diary. Toward the end, he finds
     Perry's final entry. He READS silently. We hear Perry's
     VOICE:

                    PERRY (V.O.)
     Did we not know we were to die, we
     would be children. By knowing it,
     we are given the opportunity to
     mature in spirit...

     Truman turns the page. It's BLANK. He closes the Diary.

     We CONTINUE to hear Perry's VOICE as Truman takes out a
     SNAPSHOT -- the one of Perry (at age 3) and Linda splashing
     in the puddle.

> PERRY (V.O.) (cont'd)
> Some take that opportunity. I hope
> I have...

Truman takes out a PENCIL DRAWING Perry did of him. It's
very good, though Truman looks old and weary in it.

> PERRY (cont'd)
> Life is only the father of wisdom.
> Death is the mother.

Truman finds, at the bottom of the package, his TIE. He
takes it out, clutches it.

Truman grasps for William Shawn's HAND, finds it, holds on
tightly. Shawn sits stoically, hoping no one will notice.

The CAMERA pulls back, up the aisle. Truman clutches the
tie, and holds on to Shawn's hand, for dear life.

> FADE TO BLACK.

TITLE UP: (each title fades up in succession)

In Cold Blood made Truman Capote the most famous writer in
America.

He never finished another book.

The epigraph he chose for his last published work reads:
"More tears are shed over answered prayers than unanswered
ones."

He died in 1984 of complications due to alcoholism.

END OF MOVIE

Q & A s

WITH DAN FUTTERMAN
AND BENNETT MILLER

On December 13, 2005, Rob Feld interviewed Dan Futterman in Los Angeles.

You've worked as an actor for years, but what was it about the Capote story that grabbed you enough to decide to write it for your first screenplay?

Dan Futterman: It was almost incidental at first that the movie was about Truman Capote, if you can believe that. I had read Janet Malcolm's book *The Journalist and the Murderer,* in which she talks about the complex, sometimes fraught relationship between a journalist and a subject, about the fact, according to her, that there's an inherent duplicity in that relationship. For the journalist, while there may be a genuine affection for the subject, there's also a driving ambition to write a great story. For the subject, there's the need to be portrayed in the best light, an understandable desire to get his story told in the most sympathetic way. Malcolm feels that the journalist always plays off of that desire on the part of the subject—always—whether he admits it or not. That's interesting to me.

I happened to read Gerald Clarke's biography of Capote right on the heels of rereading Malcolm's book. This was about six or seven years ago. Clarke devotes two long chapters to the period in Capote's life during which he was writing *In Cold Blood,* during which he developed this deeply complex relationship with Perry Smith. I thought: this is it—this is what I want to write about. Of course, the more I read about Truman Capote, the more I realized that he's in fact an incredible subject for a film –complex, funny, extremely verbal, a man with powerful drives—that I'd been genuinely lucky in choosing him to write about. Capote had mixed motivations for being involved with Perry—on the one hand a genuine caring for him, while on the other a purely mercenary interest in him. That relationship, in particular the way in which it ended, had devastating consequences for Capote. That period turned out to be the pivot in his life. He got everything he ever wanted, became more famous and wealthy and respected than he could ever have dared to imagine, and lost himself in the process.

It always strikes me that there's some journalism in doing a biographical film, as well, and some responsibility, though not absolute, to get things right.

DF: I think that's right. The crafting of the story is a complicated thing because you simply can't be entirely stringent in terms of chronology. You want to be careful, though, and not stray very far from the literal truth. In that way it was important to have Gerald Clarke as a sort of adviser/resource/godfather/friend of the project. It was important to have him say to me, "This is okay, I was friends with Truman, and that's him, that's how he behaved."

You clearly didn't want this to look like a standard biopic.

DF: I find many of them to be reductionist, with a few notable exceptions. They often follow this formula of showing, at the beginning of the movie, the seminal events in childhood or young adulthood that made the man the person he became. I mean, if it was that simple I wouldn't have spent seven years in therapy. I wish it was that simple.

So you had the theme you wanted to explore. Did you always have this piece of his life bracketed off?

DF: It was clear that this was the story. In 1959, Capote had achieved a certain level of fame and he wasn't satisfied with it. He was casting around for the next thing to write and, while he was overtly ready to dive into it artistically, he was also covertly ready for the book that came out of it to take him to the next level. In my reading of him, I think that was always on his mind. His engine of ambition was always running. It's a eureka moment for Capote when he reads the article about the Clutter killings. I knew I wanted to have that at the beginning of the movie, that eureka moment, reading the article in *The New York Times.* I also knew how the movie would end. I had this image of him in the first-class section of a plane, flying back to New York—and to everything the publication of the book would bring—after witnessing the execution. That would be the end. It was everything in the middle I had to figure out.

You had never written a screenplay before. What was your process of figuring out what, exactly, that is?

DF: It took me a very long time because I was trying to learn how to do it while I was doing it. When I started, my writing was completely haphazard. I didn't know if I was going to write a play or a screenplay, but I knew that I was most interested in that relationship between Truman and Perry. So I just started writing these random scenes of them talking about "interesting things," but that wasn't working at all, so I scrapped it. I had to figure out a way into it. I met my now wife, Anya Epstein, who is a terrific writer and who was, at the time, writing for the TV show *Homicide*. She was so helpful, so explicit with me that I needed to first write a detailed outline that didn't have any "talking about interesting things." I needed to be strict about it—it had to be all plot. Now, this is a movie about a writer writing a book, so to divine the plot out of this six-year period was essential. It took me a long time to do, probably a year of on-and-off writing, and showing it to her and talking about it. It was incredibly illuminating to write the outline, and it enabled me to figure out exactly what the story was that I was telling. This is probably perfectly obvious to anyone who's written a screenplay before. I hadn't. I realized through that process that I was writing a movie about a man's ambition winning out over the better parts of himself.

I know you developed it a good deal with Bennett, but what was your first draft like?

DF: I think to call it a first draft probably doesn't quite describe it because I was so scared, while I was writing, of driving down a dead end and being unable to back out of it—I'd write pages ten to fifteen and then go back to page one and make sure everything worked from there, then write another five pages and go back to page one. So it was really more like a twentieth draft by the time I got through.

The greatest changes as a result of working with Bennett were tonal shifts, but they were extremely important. The way I had written the script, it was divided into first and second halves, the first half being that, after Truman reads the *New York Times* story, he and his friend, Harper Lee, go on this adventure to Kansas—it's exciting, it's scary, they've never done this kind of thing before, and Truman Capote's like a fish out of water, having a terrible time fitting in with the folks in Garden City. That was the first half—lots of hijinks. Then, the second half: Perry is arrested and brought to Kansas and everything changes.

What Bennett said to me is that he thought that I was seeing the story the way Capote probably saw it, which was that he was a victim of circumstance, the circumstance being that Perry entered his life and changed everything. What Bennett wanted us to be clear about was that this was a story about Capote's ambition being awakened; that, in the way that a character from a Greek tragedy has a fatal flaw that he must confront, Capote was destined to confront himself—and his ambition—through Perry, the moment he got on the train to Kansas. Tonally, the entire screenplay became much more of a piece. We cut down significantly on the fish-out-of-water business. We tried to get the first act as short as possible before Perry comes in.

Capote is such an extravagant character. How did you approach putting him on-screen and keeping him believable?

DF: A lot of that was Phil simply being a genius, that's a lot of it. His performance is remarkable. There's a sobriety to his performance—it's incredibly grounded—which, in turn, only serves to highlight the flamboyant, more outlandish aspects of Truman's character. Phil seems to have an innate sense of how to structure a performance: what to let out when, and how much is needed. You read these accounts of people meeting Capote for the first time, and the general reaction is that he just did not seem like a real person at first. People were astounded by this outlandish voice and fey manner—particularly at a time when hardly anyone was allowing themselves, was brave enough, to behave like that. Quickly, though, they'd get used to the voice and forget about the mannerisms, and they'd realize how deeply intelligent and perceptive and utterly charming he was. I think that the audience has that same experience watching Phil's performance. The first scene at the party—I've seen the movie eight times now, and every time I see it I have the same reaction: *Does a person really behave like this? Is that possibly sustainable?* But then, almost instantly, you forget about the externals and begin to be captivated by the person underneath. Phil's achievement is just enormous.

It's also a bit more permissible for him to be so big in that opening scene because he's literally performing, and you see him as the attention-craving guy he was.

DF: Absolutely. I also think that, looking back on that scene, aside from how charming, smart, socially hooked up, and captivating he is, you get a sense of that ambition, that need to be laughed at, laughed with, appreciated. That was a scene we did in reshoots. We had always put a pin in that one: What's the introduction to Capote? I probably have eight versions of that scene—at a Jazz Club, walking on the street, in Truman's backyard, talking about different things with different people—till we finally got to that one, and shot it months later. Bennett and I talked repeatedly about what was needed from that scene, how much was needed, and what subjects should be discussed.

How did you envision the aesthetic of the film as you wrote it? It has a documentary-type feel, in certain places. Did you think about that?

DF: A little bit. I know that Adam Kimmel [the director of photography] and Bennett have, over the years, developed a certain aesthetic together, which I think was perfect for this film. They shot it with a very short depth of field and not a tremendous amount of information in the frame, so they could direct your attention to what they wanted to highlight. There's a lot of overlap, aesthetically, in terms of what I had imagined or hoped for—which is wonderful.

I think I knew that Bennett would do such tremendous work directing this film because, besides knowing him and talking about movies and art and everything else under the sun for twenty-five years, I know his work as a documentary filmmaker. There's a way to make this movie that's a really bad way to make it, in a sort of subjective fashion that idolizes or otherwise comments on Capote. I knew that Bennett has an objective way of approaching material. When he was making *The Cruise*, he ended up with some insane amount of footage—a hundred hours or more—and editing it was a question of him watching and watching and watching, just running through all that material repeatedly and letting the movie bubble up from that. There's something about this film that needed that same kind of attention and patience and deep sensitivity, but also objective distance.

Each character in the film is very specific and well characterized. You're an actor and come from a perspective of taking on a character and developing it yourself. How did that impact your writing of them?

DF: I've also played a lot of small parts, so I'm sort of sensitive to that. I know that you can score with small parts, so I tried to give the small characters as much drive and motivation as the lead character in the scene. I've spent my career trying to do that as an actor, so I think it felt natural, as a writer, to do that. For example, the Warden—I knew that the story was going to be that Capote bribes him, but what else can I add to it? That he's running for Congress and that's why he's talking to Capote; he wants to get a little publicity. Stuff like that felt important to me, to give people something to play.

David Hare said he wants to give every actor a reason to be in the theater. He doesn't want anyone to have a boring night onstage.

DF: I've been there, it's terrible. You know the part is just there to help illuminate something about the main character, and you feel like a water carrier.

The story obviously takes place outside of your world, in 1950s Kansas. You come from the Northeast, outside of New York. Had you ever spent time there? Did you go research the area?

DF: I drove cross-country with my wife six years ago—we stopped in Monroeville, Alabama, where Truman grew up, in the house next to Harper Lee. What I found is that the country is so changed, it's nothing like it was back in 1959. There are 7-11's on the corner, mini-marts. I read through all of the court testimony and the letters between Capote and the Deweys. I think I was helped much more by my reading than by travel. The fifty years between the early sixties and now have been tremendously impactful; places are just not what they were.

There are differences, but the country has replicated itself from coast to coast.

DF: That's right. I think that it wound up being fortunate that we shot in Canada because the towns outside of Winnipeg don't have the 7-11's or Starbucks. There's a lot of that part of Canada that seems as if it's from that time.

You had a complex constellation of characters, each relating to one another in a different way and much of it under the surface. How did you approach how these characters would interact with Capote—sometimes placating him, sometimes not, sometimes needing approval from him—and balancing that with what you had to have the audience experience from this character, from Capote?

DF: I think dealing with Perry was clear to me because it was clear what Perry needed from Truman. The real juggling act was with Nelle Harper Lee and Jack Dunphy. It's an amazing thing about Capote, I think, that while he was such a social person, and so focused on his status in society in general and literary society in particular, he was best friends with two famously reclusive people, one of whom was really misanthropic. By all accounts, Jack Dunphy hated everybody. That was interesting to me.

The problem was that I was concerned that Jack and Harper Lee might end up having the same attitude toward the journey Truman was on, the same concern for him and his soul as he got deeper and deeper into it. I think they probably did, to some extent. But I also made an effort to decide how their concern for him would be different, how it would be differently expressed and what Capote would express to each of them. Something that ended up being helpful was realizing that at that point, professionally, after Harper Lee had that huge success with *To Kill a Mockingbird*, Truman was kind of situated in the middle of the two of them, professionally. So there were probably things which he was more comfortable talking about with Nelle than with Jack, and there were jealousies going on, on all sides.

If they were redundant, one character would have to disappear.

DF: Exactly. There was also some hinting at the jealousy from Jack toward the relationship that Truman had with Perry. I tried to express that, but not dwell on it. There was one very big part of Capote's life that we hardly touched on, his whole relationship with the "Swans" in New York. These beautiful women whom he eventually betrayed—Gloria Guiness and Babe Paley and the rest—but there was just no room for it.

Those two tall, beautiful women in that first party scene? That's who they are. But nobody realizes it is them.

Perry must have been an interesting character to construct. He's a brutal murderer and you don't want to make him too sympathetic, but he is being exploited and victimized in his own way, and you do want to humanize him.

DF: Right. Almost immediately, Capote was fascinated by this beautiful, probably dangerous, enigmatic man. Perry reads, he uses these big words, and he's wary of Capote as Capote endeavors to get close to him. Perry didn't have the wherewithal to defend and insulate himself from the world, and certainly not from the likes of Truman Capote. His need for his new friend was so powerful that he kept coming back for more, despite all the signs that Capote had begun to tire of him, and to use him.

While I was writing the script, I had this image of a puppy who gets smacked by its owner, only to come crawling back and try to nuzzle up to him again. This dynamic works most vividly in the climactic scene between Truman and Perry—the scene in which Perry finally tells Truman the details of what happened that night at the Clutters. The scene begins with Perry furious at Truman, having just learned the details of Capote's reading at the 92nd Street Y, a reading at which the title of Capote's book-in-progress was revealed: *In Cold Blood*. Capote's manipulation of Perry is so complete that at the very moment when Perry is the most deeply hurt and angry with him, Capote gets him to finally reveal that last bit of information which Capote's been waiting four years to hear.

There's something else I love about that scene—and it's something that Bennett and I talked about repeatedly. I knew, when I was writing the screenplay, that I wanted, at the moment the audience is feeling the most sympathetic toward Perry—the most caring toward him because it's become abundantly clear by now that Truman is using and manipulating him—to remind the audience in a vivid, shocking way of the violence at the heart of this man. I had written into the script that there should be flashes of the night of the crime on the screen as Perry recounts that bloody night to Truman. The open question, though, was at what point those flashbacks should start. I think that Bennett chose the perfect place for this. Perry is telling Truman about the night of the killings, about how he thought Mr. Clutter was a very nice gentleman, and that he thought so right up to the moment he cut his throat. It's such an odd way for Perry to say that he killed Mr. Clutter, and it takes a moment for the audience to absorb exactly what it is that he's said. For a moment we're caught up in Perry's confusion and sorrow and surprise over what he'd done to Herb Clutter, and that's the very moment that we see, for the first time, the violence on-screen. It's a shocking image, of Herb Clutter on the cellar floor with his throat cut, and it's an enormously effective choice by Bennett to show it at this particular moment. All at once we're reminded of the disturbed and violent nature of Perry Smith, a man for whom we've been feeling tremendous sympathy.

Bennett was a friend of yours, but was there another reason why you brought the project to him? Did you feel that he would get this character and situation particularly well?

DF: I've known in some way for twenty-five years how talented Bennett is. He also has a different perspective on things than I do. I think I sensed that would be helpful to me as a writer. I knew that Bennett has an innate sense of how to put together a movie, what's effective and what's not. He knows how to shoot a movie. What I didn't know is how great he would be with the actors; he was tremendous. There aren't just one or two great performances in this movie, there are twenty great performances, all through the film, and that's all credit to Bennett. Being close friends with Bennett since high school—and the two of us having met and become friends with Phil at that time—it was always a fantasy that we would work together on something; we both knew that Phil was the perfect person to do this part. Get Phil to do it and we could all do it together.

In Bennett's **The Cruise,** *Speed is this very outsider, eccentric guy.*
DF: Perry's also like that.

Insiders and outsiders.
DF: That's right.

Is that something that you decided to play into, also, or did that come later?
DF: I don't think I had really articulated that to myself. I knew that Capote was fascinated by Perry, I knew that he was attracted to him, that he was drawn to the violent part of Perry's nature, that he felt as if they

had had very similar childhoods, that they'd been damaged in similar ways, that they both had artistic aspirations—one successful, one not. Bennett was the first person to say the word to me: outsiders. I don't know whether it actually changed anything concretely in the writing, but it just gave me so much clarity about it. These were two outsiders; that's what it was, that's what he saw in him. One had been successful in making that work for him. One hadn't. That was the connection.

It's funny the way you can sometimes only discover what you've actually written later. Were there things you learned about your writing from this freshman experience?

DF: There's a script idea that I've been fooling around with about the notion of unintended consequences: good motives turned bad, dangerous drives that people have. I guess writing *Capote* helped articulate to me what it is that I'm actually interested in writing.

A darker underbelly to things?

DF: I don't know. Maybe I have a slightly pessimistic or negative view of human motivations; mostly selfish, rarely magnanimous. I guess I do have that feeling of a darker underbelly to many stories. Not to say that there aren't very good people in the world, but they don't tend to make the best subjects for movies.

★ ★ ★

On December 13, 2005, Rob Feld also met with Bennett Miller in Los Angeles.

You've known your collaborators on* Capote *for quite some time.
Bennett Miller: I've known Danny since we were twelve. We grew up in Westchester together. Danny and I met Phil when we were all sixteen at a theater program we all did over the summer.

Did you go to school for film?
BM: I tried it. I lasted about a year and a half in NYU's film program before dropping out.

Was it just not doing it for you?
BM: Bad student, in general. I always struggled in school.

How did you proceed, then?
BM: I got an internship with Jonathan Demme that turned into an assistant job. That lasted about a year. I learned a good amount before getting fired. That was the last regular job I ever had. What followed was a lot of scrounging around. I did a no-budget music video for some friends, which got me some real music videos, but that wasn't my thing and it didn't go too far. I did odd jobs, started directing corporate industrials… I did some little documentaries that were used by not-for-profits to raise money. The truth is that I was twelve years old when I began fantasizing about working in film, and I found myself in my mid-twenties blindly pursuing that goal. I wasn't happy. I didn't like what I was doing. I stopped and re-evaluated. I decided to get out of film. Exposure to non-profits turned me on to the notion of public service of some kind, and I decided that that was what I was going to do: help the homeless, or something.

But, of course, the moment I made that decision something happened. I had relieved myself of ambition and all the distortions it causes a person. I had been blindly pursuing and trying and wanting. The moment I relieved myself of that, I experienced a kind of rebirth. When you say to yourself, "I can walk away from this. I don't need anything at this moment," you get a fearlessness. That's when clarity avails itself. It's impossible to be inspired with all that noise. I was operating under the belief that I needed permission or approval of some kind to do what I wanted to do, so much so that I wasn't really in touch with what that was. Giving up that *mishegoss* put me face-to-face with something I really did want to do.

Which was The Cruise. *How did you find Timothy "Speed" Levitch? He's an amazing character.*

BM: I'd known him for some time. It had occurred to me in the past to make a documentary portrait. In the years before Speed, there were two people who interested me in this way. Both were outsiders and homeless, like Speed. Both ended up dying, actually, in different ways. I had come to regret not having made the effort. And then there was Speed, who was somebody, at that time, really struggling on the edge of oblivion. It happened in that particular moment, when I was letting go of my goals, that *The Cruise* was just sitting there. There was a clarity and a simplicity about it. And I said, "Before I quit and go off to this other world, I'm just going to do this one thing and make sense of my years of thinking about and dabbling with film." I didn't need much to do it. I had just read about these digital cameras that were about to come out and found a way of getting one before they released them. It was the VX-1000, one of the first mini-DV cameras. I think the serial number was like 000000000143. I shot, produced, and directed it myself. Everything I needed to shoot it fit in a knapsack—that, and a pocketful of subway tokens.

How did you handle sound?

BM: I found a company in Canada that made this little adapter that you screw onto the bottom of your camera that enables the use of real mikes. So, Speed had a wireless and I had a shotgun mike mounted on the camera, and I mixed it myself. Of course, the moment *The Cruise* was done, all those doors I had been banging on began to open.

So, let's talk about Speed a little bit. He's a particularly idiosyncratic character. Pretty out there. Where did you meet him?

BM: He had gone to high school with my little brother—Speed was only twenty-five when I shot the movie; most people think he's so much older.

I'm really interested in his preoccupation with structures of civilization and how we/he exists in and outside of them. He feels himself to be an outsider, which seems to be the type of character you're drawn to.

BM: Yes. He's an outsider by nature, and outsiders are always interesting to me. When I encounter somebody who is actually an individual, I come alive. You can't be an actual individual and not have an original perspective on life, a perspective that's not lazy. It's where creativity and insight come from, from getting outside of common thought. There's also a loneliness there that's interesting, and a dichotomy that often happens; their necessity to relate to the world causes them to establish a kind of charisma that's more like a counterpart to a more difficult internal experience. Often there's a talent associated with it, a gift and an intelligence. This is true with both Truman and Speed. It was not within their constitution to conform. From the time they were crawling, they were crawling in a weird way. They both have strange voices. They both turned to writing and became obsessed with expressing themselves in a way that transcended the personal signals that they naturally emit.

It is an interesting dichotomy. Speed talks about and attempts to be an individual, to be original, and yet there's that need to be loved and accepted by the mainstream.

BM: Yeah. He talks about how some people like to appreciate the beauty of flowers, and some people like to become the flower.

And he wants to be loved by the flower.

BM: Yes. He doesn't want to be separate. But I'm not really that interested in the whole "ordinary people in extraordinary circumstances" angle. I'm interested in people who are pioneering and exploring and find themselves out there in situations that are more a consequence of their character and of who they are, than stories of people who find themselves in random circumstances. Everybody rants about conformity, but it's true. It is a kind of disease, and it's hard to fight. The oxygen is very thin up there when you're really apart from it and, when you can't buy into it, it requires you to be alive and present and thinking and surviving and creating.

All of your subjects, from your films to commercials, are extremely well characterized. From the first seconds you're gripped by, and have a tangible sense of, them. Do you remember how we meet Speed in the film?

BM: Speed is introduced as a curiosity. Over black you hear his odd voice struggling through Gershwin's "But Not for Me." We fade in to reveal a figure, which only further provokes the question, "What the hell am I looking at?" As the film progresses there is the attempt to fuel curiosity while peeling back the layers until ultimately we reach something unexpectedly moving. *Capote* is similar, beginning with the public facade and peeling back to the more disturbing reality behind the charisma. It was a breakthrough for me when I started seeing *Capote* as more of a portrait than a story. The story is there and it's essential, but the treatment of the subject gives emphasis to character over story. Story serves the purpose of revealing character and not the other way around. The challenge with Capote was to provoke that intrigue about his character from the very beginning and to sustain it throughout the film. A lot of effort was made to organize the first act in such a way that every scene revealed a different aspect of Truman's character. There's a lot to this person, and the idea here was to let you know there's a lot more to him than meets the eye.

It's a fragmented persona presenting a multifaceted human being.

BM: Yes. And the whole style of the film attempts to do the same thing: to intimate a world beneath the surface. The very first shot of the film attempts to do this. It's a shot of wheat stalks being blown in the wind that lasts longer than one expects it to. What this does, hopefully, is allow you to have a literal experience... i.e., "That's wheat ... we're in the Midwest," or whatever. And *then,* when the shot doesn't cut away, to begin to experience the actual aesthetics of it—the sound ... the color ... the age—and begin to feel what it's communicating on a subtler, nonliteral level. By holding that shot, there's a statement that the film is making: that there's more here than you're seeing, and pay attention.

It's maintaining a question.

BM: Yes, always. Even though *The Cruise* has less of a structure in the first act than this movie does, it's the same thing. It's the same concept.

With The Cruise, *when did you find the story that you wanted to tell? Did you know him so well that you knew how it would unfold? Or did you really just discover it while you were shooting?*

BM: I always knew what I wanted the film to communicate. How it would do it, I left open. *Capote* was similar. I knew what I wanted the film to deliver, but even going into it, you don't know how it's going to happen. The movie has got to communicate a great deal and it has to do it on many levels, and it's not totally evident, going in, how. I'm comfortable, though, with a process that allows for exploration and discovery throughout.

How much is that in the collaboration between your actors and writers, because you're obviously not in it alone?

BM: Collaboration is essential. The kind of solutions that come from a body of talent working together have a quality I prefer to what one person can contrive alone, and manipulate out of actors.

I'm wondering if you took something from the commercial experience, where you have so little time and you have to communicate something so immediately. They frequently present fairly oddball characters, and you characterize them so clearly.

BM: Commercials were for me a great "wax-on, wax-off" experience. Having done dozens and dozens of commercials, I never get bored by the challenge of communicating character. Something else, though, is the attention to detail that commercial work invites. The amount of information you end up thinking about for a thirty-second spot has affected the way I read scripts for the rest of my life. When you've only got thirty seconds, the smallest things become important. You end up thinking it second to second. If a lamp is needed to sit on a table in the background of a shot, I'll look at two hundred options, because it does communicate something, and why not have it say the right thing?

You were working on another doc, weren't you? What was that?

BM: It was a portrait of a meditation teacher named S. N. Goenka. He's eighty-three years old now, from India. He came to do a tour of the U.S. in a Winnebago. I did the entire tour and shot four months on the road with him talking to audiences of varying interests, just watching that intercourse with Western minds and how it was varyingly received.

So, again, it's an incongruous meshing of worlds, personas, and worldviews.

BM: And a guy having something to offer who doesn't naturally fit in.

Did you always intend to do a narrative feature, and what was it about Capote *that you chose it as your first?*

BM: Narrative features were always the goal. After *The Cruise* I had opportunities, but I waited until it felt right. *Capote* spoke to me because I saw the opportunity to do what few films attempt and what I thought I could do, which was to make a dynamic film about such an internal experience. It's also such a sobering and relevant story.

Where did you see the problems when you first got the script? What did you develop it to?

BM: Well, I'll tell you what wasn't a problem: the story. Danny really figured out what it was, and that's no small thing. He managed to distill from Capote's life the essential beats that would add up to a great story for the screen. Most of the scenes from his first draft made it to the screen in one form or another. What I was concerned with was perspective. *How* we saw the story and *how* these scenes were to work. I did not want to tell this story so much as I wanted to observe it, and for me *how* a thing is observed is almost as important as what is being observed. So the challenge was establishing a perspective and doing it in an almost invisible way. My take on the story is that it is tragic, which is to say, inevitable and the consequence of character. Whether Perry Smith kills that family or not, Truman Capote is destined for greatness, and destined for self-destruction; your character is your destiny, and you don't need the whole life story to see how he ends up. The screenplay came to work in such a way as to make that possible. Story was cut. Scenes like Harper Lee going into the diner, getting information and overhearing stuff were replaced by tonal scenes like Capote entering the funeral parlor and looking into the caskets, to emphasize the subfrequency of the story that only Truman was attuned to. That sort of thing.

You've got two things going on: the story right on the surface, which represents public Capote, and the quieter, more tonal stuff, that represents internal, private Capote. We juxtaposed those. My mantra for the first act, and the whole movie, was, *There is something going on here and you don't know what it is.* Beyond that, it's creating a sense of tragic arc to it by saying, "The guy was so desperate for that acknowledgment and praise, he needed it to survive, and he was going to find a way to get it." He was going to find a way to destroy himself because, deep down, that yearning and desperation was a sickly thing. I wanted to make it so that these killings were some kind of a calling. That's what that music is, there. It's when he's called. She discovers that body and you hear that music radiating out. Cut to that field, which to me just communicates something. It's death. Hold on that shot for twenty seconds and just hear this music. Then you go to a cityscape of New York that complements the landscape and that music fades into a jazzier thing, and basically sows the seeds of stuff underneath. Don't start with Capote; start with that underneath. Then everybody and everything that's going on is now loaded. Nobody knows what's up with Capote. Only we are aware of the siren that's calling him. To create that in the script was new. Other than that, we just tried to simplify, space out, and create opportunities for silences, and remove as much of it as we could and still stand it on its own legs. Even then, I still probably lost a quarter or a third of it in edit.

Your two films have a rhythm to them of silences interspersed with action. We see Speed talking and talking and talking, and then quiet; we're looking at the buildings or the city, or him spinning in place, or whatever. Similarly with Capote, we see him at a frenetic party, and then quiet, or a field or something. What does that rhythm give you? Does it let people digest?

BM: Again, it's about how you watch. These films scrutinize their subjects. These rhythms are the experience of consciousness. That sounds kind of pretentious, but that's what it is. You get inside the mind of someone who is scrutinizing with real focus and sensitivity. That's how these characters need to be looked at. Also, are you familiar with [the French psychoanalyst] Jacques Lacan's notion of *scansion?* When he saw patients, he would not end the sessions based on a predetermined time limit. He would end the session unexpectedly at a point of great resonance. An analysand would say something revelatory—maybe forty minutes into a session, maybe ten minutes—and Lacan would say, "That's a good place to stop." Then you must leave with that moment and don't just turn the page on it. Filmically, how do you do that? How to scansion it? Sometimes that means cutting something short, sometimes that means extending it. But the art of it is to magnify what needs to be looked at and felt.

The relationships in **Capote** *are very complex, and so much is in the subtext. It must have been an incredible balancing act maintaining each one. I guess you have to feel it out. Is it a moment-to-moment thing, and how much of that stuff can you really block out beforehand, or how much of it is what your actors gave you at a given moment?*

BM: So much of it is discovered along the way and throughout editing. In fact, we were careful not to take it too far in rehearsal. We'd take it to a point where we felt we were close enough, but none of us wanted to get there. The first time any of these moments were to come to life would be with the cameras rolling. And then, of course, films are really made in the editing. Much of the complexity you're referring to was managed in the editing. Films are reconceived, rewritten, re-acted, redirected in the edit. Of course, it has to be in the footage to begin with, but people would be amazed at how much is conjured in the edit. But that approach of remaining open throughout produces the deepest results… I think. Maybe my process is similar to Phil's, in that Phil does like to do lots of preparation and to think things through to the nth degree. He has incredible diligence in his preparation. But when the time comes, that preparation really takes a backseat to instinct and intuition. To be alive in that moment and have the authority to say, "Fuck that. I'm going to do something totally different." He would do that, too. In one case he played a scene the exact opposite of what he said he was going to.

What scene was that? How did that work?

BM: It is when Capote says goodbye to the killers. Phil just didn't see that as an emotional scene at all. He thought that it would be too narcissistic to allow his emotions out. He's not going to cry or become emotional in front of these guys, he felt. He's going to be generous to them and not make it about himself. "They're about to fucking die, so I'm not going to get emotional" was his thing. I argued, "How do you keep your composure in this situation?" He said, "Bullshit," left the room, and closed the door. Roll cameras, he opened the door, walked in and faced the guys. Veins started bulging out of his forehead. He did everything he could do not to cry, but that's Phil. He told himself what Capote told himself, "If I'm going to go there, I'm not going to make this about myself. This is how I'm going to handle it." Then you get in the situation. He entered the room and was in the moment. He really fought against it, up until a minute before we were rolling, but in the moment he allowed the truth of the situation to take him.

Could Capote have been too over the top? How do you approach putting a character as big as Capote on-screen and keeping it believable? Did you have concerns about portraying such a caricatured individual?

BM: That was a big concern. But, you know, Phil is a great actor. Really, what's concerning about it is the potential for this profound humiliation. It could have been ridiculous. It could have been Greg Kinnear, in *Stuck on You*. That's a good movie, by the way. I saw that when we were prepping, and it gave me an anxiety attack because it reminded me of the potential for ridiculousness. But Phil wasn't putting on a character. He owned it and was able to go deep with it.

Capote and Speed are such large and compulsive characters. They're both uncontrollably drawn by who they are and, at points, are given the love they seem to crave, but do they know what to do with it, once achieved?

BM: That's the irony. It's the notion of answered prayers, which is more than a saying. Capote did get everything, but that was just a milestone on what would turn out to be a descent into hell. He did achieve greatness and he did receive the praise and recognition he had hoped such an accomplishment would bring him. He threw his famous black-and-white ball for himself, which was, in a way, the beginning of the end for him. The people he cared about had the opinion that he wanted, but it was a very inaccurate reflection of himself, according to his own self-image. He created the image in the mirror and then broke the mirror because it was bullshit. He didn't feel that way about himself. He turned on his friends and violated their confidences. He betrayed them, and in so doing caused people to feel about him more closely to the way I think he felt about himself. So he went around fabricating a reflection of himself in society that he couldn't tolerate. He didn't want to belong to the club that would have him, and then he destroyed the lie. The Clarke book is powerful in the way it describes Capote's downfall and death, with him basically shriveling up into a child again and ending where he began, calling for his mother and fantasizing about a toy he had when he was a kid.

Wow! Rosebud.
BM: It is. It's Rosebud.

You didn't go for the biopic model, though, and stopped before that moment in his life. At the end of the day, that format can show someone's whole life and yet tell you absolutely nothing. Yet in that last moment with him in the film, you see where he's going. We have such an idea of who he is.
BM: Hopefully, you do. Credit Danny for bracketing off the story within Capote's life. There was a reason to tell this story that goes beyond the specifics of one person. I was attracted to the tragic themes and wanted to serve that. Once you've really locked your focus on what that really is, it becomes evident what is needed and what is not needed to serve it. So much was able to come out. It's like that Jenga game, where you keep pulling out blocks and it keeps standing. Not only does it continue to stand, but it becomes increasingly tense to look at.

Is Freud right, you are your history—at least in narrative—and to give too much of it would hamper discovery, so you have to limit it and space it out, or is it irrelevant up to a point?
BM: The whole notion that you are your history is something I don't buy into completely. I used to date a girl who was studying to be a cognitive psychologist. That's what she wrote her thesis on, the "you-are-your-story" thing. Certainly it's important, but I think your story could just as easily threaten and prohibit somebody from seeing you. I'm wary of offering labels. The moment someone fixes in on you like that, that's it. You're put in a box and it's over. You're not looking at it anymore, it's not alive. So I would answer your question and say, Yes, you've got to be careful about how much of that you share. *The Cruise* was like a study in this. There was no biographical information in that whole movie. You don't know Speed's name, you don't see where he came from. There is no information. He talks about his grandparents for a moment and there's an angry outburst about his mother, but biographically, that was it. It's all character. It's all portraiture. But you do get a powerful and deep sense of character. I have a personal disgust for

people who have strong opinions about people they've never even met, much less about a character on a screen.

There's somebody I want to make a documentary about now. He's a public figure who is nothing like what people would imagine, or at least there is something much more profound going on. The whole idea of the documentary is to *not* tell this person's life story or history—which we all know—but to just get into the character and realize this person is in another dimension altogether. I would say it's about withholding as much as it is revealing. I feel like I learn more from you, just sitting here and getting your vibe and noticing that you compulsively tap your foot, than knowing that you went to this school, or that this or that thing happened.

The problem of trying to put something truthful on film is that, by nature, you have to home in and put your finger on something, on a character, at some point. I would think a tension exists between wanting to tell a story that is, in part, about not letting people be defined so easily but, in so doing, defining them.

BM: Exactly. That's the challenge. You're right, and these are the questions we faced in editing. You want to stop someone from becoming too sympathetic or allowing the audience to become too opposed, too condemning. But you don't want to restrict parts of the person, at the same time. I think it's about knowing what it is that you want out of the character. Where are you getting to? What are you after? For me, the final scene of the film was the destination. It's the scene with Capote on the airplane after the execution. He's sitting there and he opens up Perry's journal. He closes the journal and looks out the window. That's it. Every beat of the movie is meant to add up in that moment—talk about a silent moment!—without saying anything. Originally, it did say more. Danny had a voiceover. Capote opens up the diary and you hear Perry Smith's voice reciting a couple of passages from the diary, which helped to add things up. Then Capote looks out the window. If the movie was successful, if we did it, we knew we could just take all that out and simply have him look at the diary with nothing but the sound of the plane's engines, and perhaps a little score, and then look out the window. Hopefully, in that moment, you just see all the numbers in all the columns tally up. He's in first class in a golden cabin, above the clouds with heavenly light shining in, and yet … you know his life is over. Anyway, if you know what it is that you want out of the character, if you know why it is you're looking at the person, then I think it becomes easy to know what to include and what to exclude.

On that I'll hit the scansion button there and say, "I think that's a good place to stop."

Rob Feld is a writer and independent producer at Manifesto Films. His writings on film and interviews with such noted filmmakers as James L. Brooks, Charlie Kaufman, Bill Condon, Peter Hedges, John Turturro, Spike Jonze, Peter Jackson, David O. Russell, Darren Aronofsky, Alexander Payne, Woody Allen, David Hare, David Koepp, Shari Springer Berman, Robert Pulcini, Grant Heslov, and George Clooney appear regularly in *Written By* magazine and *DGA Magazine*, as well as in the Newmarket Shooting Script® series.

from *Capote: A Biography,* by Gerald Clarke

In describing the genesis of a successful work, a writer often will say that he stumbled across his idea, giving the impression that it was purely a matter of luck, like finding a hundred-dollar bill on the sidewalk. The truth, as Henry James observed, is usually different: "His discoveries are, like those of the navigator, the chemist, the biologist, scarce more than alert recognitions. He *comes upon* the interesting thing as Columbus came upon the isle of San Salvador, because he had moved in the right direction for it."

So it was that Truman, who had been moving in the right direction for several years, came across his San Salvador, his interesting thing, in that brief account of cruel death in far-off Kansas: he had been looking for it, or something very much like it. For no apparent reason, four people had been slain: Herbert Clutter; his wife, Bonnie; and two of their four children, Nancy, sixteen, and Kenyon, fifteen. As he read and reread those Spartan paragraphs [an account of the killings on a back page of *The New York Times*], Truman realized that a crime of such horrifying dimensions was a subject that was indeed beyond him, a truth he could not change. Even the location, a part of the country as alien to him as the steppes of Russia, had a perverse appeal. "Everything would seem freshly minted," he later explained, reconstructing his thinking at that time. "The people, their accents and attitude, the landscape, its contours, the weather. All this, it seemed to me, could only sharpen my eye and quicken my ear." Finally he said to himself, "Well, why not *this* crime? The Clutter case. Why not pack up and go to Kansas and see what happens?"

When he appeared at *The New Yorker* to show Mr. Shawn [William Shawn, the magazine's editor] the clipping, the identity of the killer, or killers, was still unknown, and might never be known. But that, as he made clear to Shawn, was beside the point, or at least the point he wanted to make. What excited his curiosity was not the murders, but their effect on that small and isolated community. "As he originally conceived it, the murders could have remained a mystery," said Shawn, who once again gave his enthusiastic approval. "He was going to do a piece about the town and the family—what their lives had been. I thought that it could make some long and wonderful piece of writing."

Truman asked Andrew Lyndon to go with him, but Andrew was otherwise engaged. Then he turned to Nelle Harper Lee. Nelle, whose own book, *To Kill a Mockingbird*, was finished but not yet published, agreed immediately. "He said it would be a tremendously involved job and would take two people," she said. "The crime intrigued him, and I'm intrigued with crime—and, boy, I wanted to go. It was deep calling to deep." Watching with some amusement as the two amateur sleuths nervously made their plans, Jack [Jack Dunphy, Capote's longtime companion] wrote his sister: "Did you read about the murder of the Clutter family out in Kansas? Truman's going out there to write a piece on it. The murder is *unsolved!!* He's taking Nelle Harper Lee, an old childhood friend, out with him to play his girl Friday, or his Della Street [Perry Mason's secretary]. I hope he'll be all right. I told him curiosity killed the cat, and he looked scared—till I added that satisfaction brought it back."

He also enlisted the aid of Bennett Cerf [his book publisher], who, he correctly assumed, had well-placed acquaintances in every state of the union. "I don't know a soul in the whole state of Kansas," he told Bennett. "You've got to introduce me to some people out there." By coincidence, Bennett had recently spoken at Kansas State University in Manhattan, Kansas, and had made a friend of its president, James McCain. By further coincidence, McCain had known the murdered Clutter family, as he did nearly everyone else in Finney County. He would give Truman all necessary introductions, he told Bennett, if, in exchange, Truman would stop first at the university to speak to the English faculty. "I accept for Truman right now," Bennett responded. "Great!"

Thus assured, in mid-December Truman boarded a train for the Midwest, with Nelle at his side and a footlocker stuffed with provisions in his luggage. "He was afraid that there wouldn't be anything to eat out there," said Nelle. After a day and a night in Manhattan, where the Kansas State English faculty gave him a party, they rented a Chevrolet and drove the remaining 270 miles to Garden City, the Finney County seat. They arrived at twilight, a month to the day after he had come upon his interesting thing in the back pages of the *Times*. But if he had realized then what the future held, Truman said afterward, he never would have stopped. "I would have driven straight on. Like a bat out of hell."

BACKGROUND NOTES

About *In Cold Blood*

With *In Cold Blood*, Capote tried to create something entirely new—what he called the "nonfiction novel." His goal was to bring the techniques of fiction—artistic selection and the novelist's eye for telling detail—to the writing of nonfiction. He wanted to prove that a factual narrative could be just as gripping as the most imaginative thriller. His success is evident on the very first page, where, with just a few words, he transports the reader to the high plains of western Kansas: "The land is flat, and the views are awesomely extensive; horses, herds of cattle, a white cluster of grain elevators rising as gracefully as Greek temples are visible long before a traveler reaches them." By the third page, when four shotgun blasts break the prairie silence, the reader is hooked. "The most perfect writer of my generation," Norman Mailer had called Capote, and *In Cold Blood* proved that Mailer had not exaggerated.

It is also hard to exaggerate the influence *In Cold Blood* was to have on other writers. Until its publication in 1966, "real" writers—writers of talent, in other words—felt they had to follow in the footsteps of Fitzgerald, Hemingway and Faulkner and write fiction. Nonfiction was for historians, journalists, and hacks. Capote opened a new path. In the decades that followed, many of the best writers in America found their subjects, just as he had done, in the gritty world of real events. Capote's influence extends even into the twenty-first century, and writers who may never have read *In Cold Blood* write the way they do because of the way he did.

The film *Capote* invites you to imagine a time when writers achieved the kind of fame and notoriety that is today associated with pop culture personalities. Americans read more in those days than they do now, and books mattered. More importantly, Truman was a natural born self-promoter who paved the way for the cult of celebrity that is omnipresent today. His fame cut across all categories, from high to low culture, from literary seriousness to high-society frivolity. His name was a constant in newspapers, magazines, and TV shows. When he walked around Manhattan, truck drivers would affectionately call to him—"Hey, Truman, how are ya?"—and long-distance telephone operators would know who he was the instant he picked up the phone.

In 1967, just a year after the book came out, director Richard Brooks went to Holcomb, Kansas, to make a film version. Avoiding Hollywood slickness, Brooks shot in black and white and cast unknowns Robert Blake and Scott Wilson as Perry Smith and Dick Hickock. However, he did cast well-known TV and film actor John Forsythe (later in *Charlie's Angels* and *Dynasty*) as Alvin Dewey. Shooting took place in the Clutter house and other real-life locations. Brooks filmed seven of the original jurors, the actual hangman, and Nancy Clutter's horse, Babe. Capote arrived during the filming, attracting enormous attention and press coverage, until Brooks, seeing him as a distraction, asked him to leave. Truman obliged, but not before he posed with Blake and Wilson for the cover of *Life* magazine.

The film opened later that year and was a great commercial and critical success. It was nominated for four Academy Awards®: Best Director and Best Adapted Screenplay (Brooks), Best Cinematography (Conrad L. Hall), and Best Music (Quincy Jones).

In Cold Blood was filmed again as a Hallmark TV movie in 1996, directed by Jonathan Kaplan *(The Accused)* and starring Sam Neill as Dewey and Eric Roberts and Anthony Edwards as Smith and Hickock. This time the filming took place in Canada.

In Cold Blood brought Capote enormous fame, money, and respect. But it also marked another turning point in his life. "In some lives," wrote Gerald Clarke, "there are moments which, looked at later, can be seen as the lines that define the beginning of a dramatic rise or decline.... The proximate cause of his tragic fall—for that's what it was—was *In Cold Blood* itself."

About Truman Capote

Novelist, short-story writer, screenwriter, playwright, creator of the "non-fiction novel," spellbinding raconteur, wit, superstar, genius, and jet-setter, all-around delight, Truman Capote was one of the most astonishing and singular personalities of his time.

He was born Truman Streckfus Persons in New Orleans on September 30, 1924. His father was Arch Persons, a small-time con man, and his mother was Lillie Mae Faulk Persons, a beautiful young woman from Monroeville, Alabama. As Lillie Mae's disappointment in Arch grew, she developed a taste for other men, and the marriage fell apart. In 1930, shortly before his sixth birthday, his parents sent Truman to Monroeville, to stay with his elderly Faulk cousins—three spinster sisters, Jennie, Callie, and Sook, and their bachelor brother, Bud. Among the Faulk cousins, Truman formed the deepest bond with Sook, who became a kind of surrogate mother. He also found friendship with the girl next door, Harper Lee, his junior by just a year. She would later portray young Truman as the character Dill in her novel *To Kill a Mockingbird*: "We came to know [him] as a pocket Merlin, whose head teemed with eccentric plans, strange longings, and quaint fancies."

His mother moved to New York City in 1931. Changing her first name to Nina, she divorced Arch, married Joseph Capote, a Cuban who worked for a textile firm on Wall Street, and brought Truman north to Manhattan. He attended the Trinity School, a private school on the West Side, and in 1935 he was formally adopted by his stepfather. Truman Persons was now Truman Capote. In 1939 the Capotes moved to Greenwich, Connecticut, a wealthy suburb of New York, and Truman attended Greenwich High School. The Capotes returned to New York in 1942 and moved into an apartment on Park Avenue. Truman, who had failed to graduate with his class at Greenwich High School, finally got his diploma from the Franklin School, a private school on the West Side, in 1943. This was to be the end of his formal education.

While attending Franklin, he took a job as the art department copyboy at *The New Yorker*. A "gorgeous apparition, fluttering, flitting up and down the corridors of the magazine," was how Brendan Gill, one of the magazine's stalwarts, described him. During a period when homosexuality was anathema in America, Truman was nonchalantly and resplendently gay.

Truman had been writing stories from an early age and he hoped that *The New Yorker* would publish him. But all his efforts were rebuffed. He found a kinder reception at two women's magazines, *Mademoiselle* and *Harper's Bazaar*, which in those days published the best short fiction in America. His first story in *Mademoiselle* was "Miriam," which not only won him an O. Henry Award but attracted great attention in Gotham's literary circles. Other stories soon followed, and in 1945 Random House gave him a contract for his first novel—*Other Voices, Other Rooms*. Unable to write at home—his mother had turned into an abusive alcoholic—Truman received a fellowship to Yaddo, a retreat for artists, writers, and composers in upstate New York.

There he began a long relationship with Newton Arvin, a professor of literature at Smith College in Northampton, Massachusetts. Twenty-four years older than Truman, Arvin was a graceful writer, a scholar of impressive erudition, and a critic of impeccable judgment. His biography of Herman Melville was to win the National Book Award for nonfiction in 1951. Both lover and father figure, Arvin, Truman later said, was also his Yale and Harvard.

Though it had only modest sales, *Other Voices, Other Rooms,* which was published in 1948, cemented Truman's reputation as one of the most promising writers of the post–World War II generation. Never explicit, it is, in fact, the story of a teenage boy's awakening knowledge of his homosexuality. It was not until much later that Capote himself was able to recognize that it was his spiritual, if not his factual, autobiography. Gerald Clarke wrote that the lead character's eccentric cousin "became the spokesman for the themes that dominate all of Truman's writing: the loneliness that afflicts all but the stupid or insensitive; the sacredness of love, whatever its form; the disappointment that invariably follows high expectation; and the perversion of innocence."

In the fall of 1948, after a summer in Europe, Truman met Jack Dunphy, a fellow writer who became his lifelong companion. In 1950 they settled in Taormina, Sicily—in a house once inhabited by D. H. Lawrence—and Truman began work on his second novel, *The Grass Harp*.

If *Other Voices, Other Rooms* was Capote's look at the dark side of his childhood, *The Grass Harp* (1951) was, in Clarke's words, "an attempt to raise the bittersweet spirits of remembrance and nostalgia." In this story of a lonely boy who finds refuge in a tree house with four other displaced spirits, Truman conjured up the memory of his childhood in Alabama and his beloved elderly cousin, Sook Faulk. Truman adapted *The Grass Harp* for Broadway the following year, but, with a run of only a month, it was not a commercial success. (A movie version, starring Walter Matthau and Sissy Spacek, was filmed in 1997.)

After doing some rewriting on the screenplay of Vittorio De Sica's *Indiscretion of an American Wife* (1952), Truman collaborated with director John Huston on the offbeat mystery-comedy *Beat the Devil* (1953). Filmed in Ravello, Italy, and starring Jennifer Jones, Humphrey Bogart, and Gina Lollobrigida, it is as quirky and light-hearted to watch as it was to make. (Capote considered his best screenplay, however, to be that of *The Innocents*, an adaptation of Henry James' *The Turn of the Screw* that was released in 1961 and starred Deborah Kerr.) After *Beat the Devil*, Jack and Truman went to Portofino, Italy, where Truman adapted his short story, "House of Flowers," into a Broadway musical. Though the score is one of Harold Arlen's best, the show had only modest success.

Truman returned to Europe, but in January 1954, he was forced to fly back to New York after his mother swallowed a bottle of sleeping pills. She died before he arrived.

Capote's interest in the possibilities of journalism led to the writing of *The Muses Are Heard*, the story of a *Porgy and Bess* troupe's visit to the Soviet Union, and "The Duke in His Domain," a long and revealing profile of Marlon Brando. After reading it, the actor professed a desire to murder him.

Truman's next book, *Breakfast at Tiffany's* (1958), created a luminescent, unforgettable heroine in Holly Golightly, a free-spirited sprite in wartime Manhattan. Holly's only anxiety is what she calls the "mean reds." Her solution: "What I've found does the most good is to just get into a taxi and go to Tiffany's," she says. "It calms me down right away, the quietness and the proud look of it: nothing very bad could happen to you there...." The film was made into a classic film directed by Blake Edwards, featuring Audrey Hepburn, Henry Mancini's song "Moon River," and a grafted-on love story. Truman, while a fan of Hepburn's, thought she had been miscast and was disappointed in the film; he felt Marilyn Monroe would have been a better choice. None of the film's legions of fans agreed with him.

In November 1959, Capote read about the Clutter murders in *The*

New York Times. Thus began *In Cold Blood* (1966), a project which would take six years of his life. Those are the years that are explored by writer Dan Futterman and director Bennett Miller in their film *Capote*.

* * *

After the long, intense years writing *In Cold Blood*, Capote gave himself a party, and on November 28, 1966, he threw one of the most spectacular bashes in the history of New York—the Black and White Ball at the Plaza Hotel. Given in honor of *Washington Post* publisher Katherine Graham, who was then the most powerful woman in the country, the gala celebration began at ten and went until breakfast the following morning. Approximately five hundred people from the most stellar reaches of the glitterati were invited, with a precise dress code: men in black tie, with black mask; women in black or white dress, white mask, plus a fan. The beau monde blowout created front-page news all over the country. "An extraordinary thing in its way," Truman said later, "but as far as I was concerned it was just a private party and nobody's business."

During the writing of *In Cold Blood*, Capote began to drink heavily and take pills. He seemed to lose focus and direct his energies more toward the high life rather than high art. He announced the title of his next novel—*Answered Prayers*—and said that it would have a scope equal to Proust's. But when the first chapter was published in *Esquire* in 1975, it unleashed an angry backlash from some of his rich friends, who were furious to see themselves portrayed as thinly disguised characters. They felt betrayed and many, including the wife of CBS chairman Bill Paley, Babe Paley, the woman he loved most of all, refused to forgive or see him. Given the nickname "The Tiny Terror," he became a social pariah, and this public shunning added to his downward spiral with drugs and alcohol.

Even his relationship with Jack Dunphy suffered, and Truman sought out affection from a series of unremarkable men. All of these relationships ended badly. Yet, with all of that, the alcohol, the drugs, and the depression, he could still write—and write very well indeed—and his last book, a collection titled *Music for Chameleons* (1980), contains prose any writer might envy.

Truman Capote died in Los Angeles on August 25, 1984, a month shy of his sixtieth birthday.

Historical Characters Portrayed in the Film

Nelle Harper Lee

A descendant of Civil War General Robert E. Lee, Nelle Harper Lee won the Pulitzer Prize for her 1960 novel *To Kill a Mockingbird*, her first and only novel. The acclaimed book featured a portrait of her Alabama childhood friend Truman Capote in the character of Dill. *To Kill a Mockingbird* was made into a successful movie in 1962, starring Gregory Peck. It was nominated for eight Academy Awards® and won three, including Best Actor for Gregory Peck. Lee went to college in Alabama and at Oxford, then moved to New York City, where she worked as an airline clerk before devoting herself to writing in the late 1950s. In 1959, Lee moved to Holcombe, Kansas, to work as a research assistant for Capote on *In Cold Blood*. Shortly after the publication of the book, Lee and Capote had a falling out and, reportedly, she did not see him for the last fifteen years of his life. After the success of *To Kill a Mockingbird*, Lee returned to her hometown of Monroeville and has only published a few short essays, although there are unconfirmed rumors that she is writing her memoirs.

Alvin Dewey Jr.

Born in 1912, Alvin Dewey Jr. was the Kansas Bureau of Investigations agent who led the investigation of the murders and a personal friend of the Clutter family. Although many other law enforcement officials from various agencies were part of the team that cracked the case, Capote made Dewey the hero of *In Cold Blood*. While Dewey said that he "came off bigger and better than life," the crime took place in his town and he coordinated the investigation. Dewey provided Capote with access to a tremendous amount of information, including entries from Nancy Clutter's diary. The Dewey family remained in contact with Truman for many years and was present at his funeral. Dewey also worked for the Kansas Highway Patrol, the FBI, and was Finney County Sheriff before joining the KBI in 1955. The stress of the Clutter case took its toll, leading to a heart attack in February 1963. Dewey retired in 1975 and died in 1987.

Perry Smith

Born October 27, 1928, in Huntington, Elko County, Nevada, Perry Edward Smith's Irish father and Cherokee mother worked the rodeo circuit as "Tex & Flo." When the riding act ended so did the marriage, as Flo began drinking and chasing other men. She took the four children and moved to San Francisco. After she died, the children were sent to orphanages. When he was sixteen, Smith joined the merchant marines and later the army, serving in Japan and Korea. Afterwards he prospected and hunted with his father in Alaska. Sensitive about his education—which stopped at third grade—Smith became obsessed with improving himself, learning to draw, play guitar, and broaden his vocabulary. A serious motorcycle accident in 1952 left him crippled, and shortly after that he received his first jail sentence, for a burglary in Philipsburg, Kansas. After his release, he joined up with Dick Hickock, a fellow "grad" of the Kansas State Penitentiary. With the exception of his sister Barbara, every member of his family died an early death, including his mother, Flo (alcoholism), brother, James (suicide), and sister Joy (fell—or jumped—out of a window).

Richard "Dick" Hickock

Born on June 6, 1931, Richard Eugene Hickock grew up in and near Kansas City with his parents and a younger brother, Walter. He was a popular student and athlete before head injuries from a serious car wreck in 1950 left him disfigured, with his eyes at slightly different levels. As Capote wrote, his head looked like it had been "halved like an apple and then put together a fraction off center." Although he had wanted to go to college, the family couldn't afford it, so he became a mechanic. He married and divorced twice, had several children, and soon began living beyond his means. He turned to check-bouncing and other petty crimes to help make ends meet, and eventually landed in prison, where he met Perry Smith.

Jack Dunphy

Born in a working-class neighborhood in Philadelphia, Jack Dunphy began his career as a dancer, and was one of the cowboys in the original Broadway production of *Oklahoma!* When he met Capote in 1948, he had written a well-received novel, *John Fury*, and was just getting over a painful divorce from musical comedy star Joan McCracken. Ten years older than Capote, Dunphy was in many ways Capote's opposite, as solitary as Truman was exuberantly social. Though they drifted more and more apart in the later years, the couple stayed together until the end. His other work includes the novels *Friends and Vague Loves, Nightmovers, An Honest Woman, First Wine,* and *The Murderous McLaughlins*, and the plays *Light a Penny Candle, Café Moon,* and *Too Close for Comfort*. Although his work consistently received good notices from critics, he never had a bestseller. In 1987 he published *Dear Genius: A Memoir of My Life with Truman Capote.*

William Shawn

Born in 1907, William Shawn (né William Chon) became the most celebrated magazine editor of the twentieth century during his thirty-five years (1952-1987) as editor of *The New Yorker.* Known for his taste, rigorous attention to detail, style, and truth, he was also famous for his quiet, self-effacing manner. During his tenure at the magazine, Shawn edited work by Truman Capote, J. D. Salinger, Philip Roth, S. J. Perelman, Ved Mehta, Harold Brodkey, E. B. White, Hannah Arendt, Edmund Wilson, Milan Kundera, Donald Barthelme, Janet Flanner, Peter Handke, and Jamaica Kincaid, to name just a few. Shawn and Cecille, his wife of sixty-three years, had two sons, the actor Wallace Shawn and the composer Allen Shawn. He also adopted a son with his mistress, writer Lillian Ross. Shawn died in 1992.

Marie Dewey

A native of New Orleans, Marie Dewey was thrilled to find out that Capote had been born there. Her desire to have a guest she could share gumbo with became Truman and Nelle's entry into the Dewey home. "Truman thinks we are genuine, sincere people," Marie Dewey said to the *Kansas City Times*. "He likes us for what we are. He became well-acquainted and fond of us over the years." Capote said that he felt that the Deweys' two boys were like his own nephews, and he encouraged the younger Alvin's writing through the mail.

CAST AND CREW CREDITS

UNITED ARTISTS and SONY PICTURES CLASSICS Present
An A-LINE PICTURES/COOPER'S TOWN
PRODUCTIONS/INFINITY MEDIA Production
PHILIP SEYMOUR HOFFMAN

CAPOTE

CATHERINE KEENER   CLIFTON COLLINS JR.   BRUCE GREENWOOD   BOB BALABAN
MARK PELLEGRINO   MARSHALL BELL   AMY RYAN   BESS MEYER and CHRIS COOPER

Casting by
AVY KAUFMAN

Music by
MYCHAEL DANNA

Costume Designer
KASIA WALICKA MAIMONE

Edited by
CHRISTOPHER TELLEFSEN, A.C.E.

Production Designer
JESS GONCHOR

Director of Photography
ADAM KIMMEL

Executive Producers
DANNY ROSETT
KERRY ROCK

Executive Producers
PHILIP SEYMOUR HOFFMAN
DAN FUTTERMAN

Produced by
WILLIAM VINCE &
MICHAEL OHOVEN

Produced by
CAROLINE BARON

Based on the book by
GERALD CLARKE

Screenplay by
DAN FUTTERMAN

Directed by
BENNETT MILLER

Associate Producers
KYLE MANN
DAVE VALLEAU

Associate Producers
KYLE IRVING
EMILY ZIFF

Canadian Casting by
COREEN MAYRS, CSA and
HEIKE BRANDSTATTER, CSA

Manitoba Casting by
JIM HEBER

Line Producer
JACQUES METHE

CAST
In Order of Appearance

Laura Kinney	. . . .	Allie Mickelson
Nancy Clutter	. . . . . .	Kelci Stephenson
Truman Capote	. .	Philip Seymour Hoffman
Christopher	. . . .	Craig Archibald
Barbara	. . . .	Bronwen Coleman
Rose	. . . .	Kate Shindle
Grayson	. . . .	David Wilson Barnes
Williams	. . . .	Michael J. Berg
Nelle Harper Lee	. . . . .	Catherine Keener
Porter	. . . .	Kwesi Ameyaw
Car Rental Agent	. . . . .	Andrew Farago
Courthouse Guard	. . . . .	Ken Krotowich
Alvin Dewey	. . . .	Chris Cooper
Roy Church	. . . .	R.D. Reid
Harold Nye	. . . . . .	Robert McLaughlin
Sheriff Walter Sanderson	. . .	Harry Nelken

Journalists	. . . .	Jon Ted Wynne
		Jonathan Barrett
		Christopher Read
Old Man	. . . .	Edward Sutton
Girls	. . . .	Mia Faircloth
		Ainsley Balcewich
Danny Burke	. . . .	Kerr Hewitt
Jack Dunphy	. . . . . .	Bruce Greenwood
Warren Hotel Desk Clerk	. .	John Warkentin
Marie Dewey	. . . .	Amy Ryan
Alvin Dewey Jr.	. . . .	Avery Tiplady
Paul Dewey	. . . . . .	Nazariy Demkowicz
Pete Holt	. . . .	John Destry
Perry Smith	. . . .	Clifton Collins Jr.
Dick Hickock	. . . .	Mark Pellegrino
Dorothy Sanderson	. . . . .	Araby Lockhart
Judge Roland Tate	. . . .	John Maclaren
Franklin Weeks	. . . .	Olie Alto
William Shawn	. . . .	Bob Balaban
Richard Avedon	. . . . . .	Adam Kimmel

Jury Foreman . . . . . Jeremy Dangerfield
Ben Baron . . . . David Rakoff
NY Reporter. . . . . Robert Huculak
Young Prison Guard . . . . . James Durham
Warden Marshall Krutch . . . Marshall Bell
Prison Guard . . . . Frank Filbert
ND Prison Guards . . . . . . Boyd Johnson
Don Malboeuf
Cruiser . . . . Will Woytowich
Lowell Lee Andrews . . . . . C. Ernst Harth
Row Guards . . . . Wayne Nicklas
Jason Love
Literary Enthusiast. . . . . Norman Armour
Linda Murchak. . . . . Bess Meyer
Herb Clutter . . . . Manfred Maretzki
Bonnie Clutter . . . . Miriam Smith
Kenyon Clutter . . . . . . Philip Lockwood
Operator . . . . . . Marina Stephenson Kerr
Chaplain. . . . . Jim Shepard
Stunt Coordinator . . . . Scott Ateah
Perry Smith Stunt Double . . Dan Redford
Produced with the participation of
MANITOBA FILM & SOUND
Unit Production Managers . . . Ellen Rutter
Caroline Baron
First Assistant Directors. Ronaldo Nacionales
Richard O'Brien Moran
Second Assistant Director . . Charles Crossin
Third Assistant Director. . . Megan Basaraba
Supervising Sound Editor. . . . Ron Bochar
Re-Recording Sound Mixers . Mark Berger
Ron Bochar
Bill Sheppard
Executive in Charge of Post Production
. . . . Stuart Burkin
Music Supervisor . . . . Susan Jacobs
Art Director . . . . Gordon Peterson
Set Decorators. . . . . Maryam Decter
Scott Rossell
First Assistant Camera . . . . Patrick Stepien
Second Assistant Camera . Robert W. Devitt
Camera Trainee . . . . Tim Connell
Still Photographer . . . . Attila Dory
Script Supervisor . . . . Alanna Mills
Production Coordinator. . . Tamara Mauthe
Production Accountant. . . . Adeline Elias
Chief Lighting Technician. . . . . John Barr
Assistant Chief Lighting Technician
. . . . Robert Rowan
Lead Electric. . . . . John Clarke
Chief Rigging Electrician. . Michael Drabot
Assistant Rigging Electrician . Jeremy Milmine
Electrics . . . . Nicolas Philips
Ryan Beresford, Nathaniel Vince

Generator Operator . . . . . Marc Gagnon
Key Grip . . . . Francoise Balcaen
Dolly Grip . . . . Owen Smith
Second Company Grip . Dominique Balcaen
Lead Grip . . . . Roger Wiebe
Key Rigging Grip . . . . . Darren Lannoo
Second Company Rigging Grip
. . . . Christopher Gower
Grips . . . . Greg Crawford
Terry Thiessen
Miles Vince
Location Manager . . . . . Bernie Narvey
Location Manager (Prep). . Carmen Lethbridge
Assistant Location Manager. . . Cliff Sumter
Off-Set Assistant Location Managers
. . . . Michael Cowles
Sarah Jane Cundell
First Assistant Editor. . . . John Sosnovsky
Sound Effects Editor . . . . Sean Garnhart
Assistant Sound Editor . . Alexa Zimmerman
Dialogue Editor . . . . . Nicholas Renbeck
ADR Editor . . . . Marissa Littlefield
Sound Mix Technician. . . . Bill Sheppard
Sound Mix Recordist . . . . Brody Ratsoy
Foley Editor . . . . Kam Chan
Foley Artist . . . . Marko Costanzo
Foley Recordist . . . . George Lara
Sound Post Production . . . . . . C5, Inc.
DBC Sound, Inc.
Production Sound Mixer . . . Leon Johnson
Boom Operator . . . . Stan Mak
FTM Sound Trainee . . . . . Sacha Rosen
Music Composed and Produced by
. . . . Mychael Danna
Orchestration by . . . . . . Nicholas Dodd
Mychael Danna
Conducted by . . . . Nicholas Dodd
Piano. . . . . Eve Egoyan
Music Editors . . . . Jennifer Dunnington
Rich Walters
Musicians Contractor . . . . Lenny Solomon
Music Recorded and Mixed by . Ron Searles
Assistant Engineers . . . . . Dennis Patterson
Charles Ketchabaw
Assistant to the Composer. . . Margo Massie
Recorded at . . . The Glenn Gould Theatre,
CBC, Toronto
Assistant Costume Designers Patti Henderson
Nadine Falk
Set Costume Supervisor . . Michelle Boulet
Truck Costumer . . . . . . Heather Neale
Extras Costume Coordinator. . Paula Dunfield
Costume Assistant . . . . Carolyn Bradshaw

IA Costume Trainee . . . . . Amy Sztulwark
FTM Costume Intern . . . . . Ben Raine
Key Make-Up. . . . . Pamela Athayde
First Assistant Make-Up. . . . Mandy Kuryk
Second Assistant Make-Up/IA Trainee
. . . . Brenda Magalas
Special Effects Make-Up Artist
. . . . Doug Morrow
Special Effects Make-Up Assistant
. . . . Brad Proctor
Key Hair . . . . Aldo Signoretti
First Assistant Hair . . . . Marcelle Genovese
Second Assistant Hair . . . . . Barry Olafson
Property Master . . . . Mark Stratton
Assistant Property Master . . . Ryan Berzuk
Props Buyer . . . . Kim Hamin
Art Department Coordinator . Holly Moore
Graphic Artist . . . . Greg Gardner
Art Department Assistant . . Kristin Tresoor
Lead Dresser . . . . Lindsey Bart
Set Dressers . . . . Alexis Labra
Remi Verfaille
Michaela Vince
On-Set Dresser . . . . Jason Wilkins
Sets Buyer. . . . . Gerry Gyles
Construction Coordinator. . . . . Olaf Dux
Head Carpenter. . . . . Mike Jansen
Key Scenic Artist . . . . . Lloyd Brandson
Paint Foreman . . . . William Baker
Scenic Artist . . . . Simon Hughes
Key Greens . . . . Burkhard Weiss
Painter . . . . Michael Madill
Mechanical Special Effects Coordinator
. . . . Mark Gebel
First Assistant Special Effects . . Tim Harding
Transportation Coordinator . . . John Mysyk
Transportation Captains
. . . . Garry (Diesel) Trosky
James Alexander
Ron Mymryk
Picture Vehicle Assistant . . . Blaine Laschuk
Picture Vehicle Driver . . . . . . Ernie Buck
Camera Car Operator . . . Paul de Bourcier
Unit Publicist . . . . Leslie Stafford
Script Researcher . . . . . Dan Chamberlin
Legal Services. . Sue Bodine, Andrew Hurwitz
Epstein, Levinsohn, Bodine,
Hurwitz & Weinstein, LLP
Production Counsel
. . . . Eva Schmieg, Heenan Blaikie
Assistant Production Coordinators
. . . . Colleen Wowchuck
Paul Hurst
First Assistant Accountant . Crystal Mikoluff

Accounting Clerks. . . . . . Ruby Alcantara
Jolyn Hoogstraten
Post Production Accountant. . . . . Jon Bell
Post Production Clerk . . . . Cherie Whyte
Infinity Production Executives
. . . . Michael Potkins
Robert Merilees
Assistant to Bennett Miller . . Zeke Hawkins
Assistants to Caroline Baron. . . Mika Taylor
Guy Penini
Assistant to Philip Seymour Hoffman
. . . . Sara Murphy
Assistant to William Vince . . . Pete Valleau
Executive Assistant to Michael Ohoven
. . . . Jereme Watt
Assistant to Jacques Méthé & William Vince
. . . . Dianne Domaratzki
Casting Associate . . . . Elizabeth Greenberg
Canadian Casting Associate . . Errin Clutton
Winnipeg Casting Assistant . . . Joey Ritchie
Key Set Production Assistant . . Emily Drake
Key Locations Production Assistants
. . . . Dimitrius Sagriotis
Amanda Smart
Locations Scout Production Assistant
. . . . Milt Bruchanski
Locations Production Assistant. . Hope Oketayot
Production Assistants . . . . . Khali Wenaus
Anne Dawson
FTM Production Office Intern . . Rhia Alcantara
New York Production Interns. . . Alex Berg
Caroline Coskren
Michael Diamond
Jacklyn Gauci
Emily McMaster
Dan Proctor
Annie Wong
Extras Casting. . . . . Lori Stefaniuk
Extras Casting Assistants . . . . Patricia Kress
Holly Rose
Catering Chef . . . . Brent Prockert
Sous Chef. . . . . Kristian Sullivan
Third Assistant Caterer . . . . . . Ryan Cyr
Key Craft Service/First Aid. . . Denys Curle
Craft Service Assistant. . . . . . Kelly Ditz
Head of Security . . . . Wayne Glesby
Security . . . . Tony Braga

THE PRODUCERS WISH TO THANK:

hungry man inc.

SPECIAL THANKS

Paul Thomas Anderson
Richard Avedon
Kenny Boyce
Jennifer Dundas
Tracey Durning
Empire Entertainment
Anya Epstein
David Feldman
Tony Greco
Helen Huffner Vintage Clothing
Glenn Horowitz Bookseller, Inc.
Warren Hooper
Kevin Hyman
Davien Littlefield
Chris McGarry
J.B. Miller
Sally Morrison
Louise O'Brien Moran
Mimi O'Donnell
Stephen Orent
Nick Ratner
Tom Rossano
Elizabeth Smith
Jeff Stamp
Russell Stetler
Norma Stevens
Stony Mountain Penitentiary
Charlie Tammaro
Nick VanAmburg
Carole Vivier
Sarah Vowell
Anthony Weintraub

Title Design by
. . . . Tröllback + Company NY-LA
Optical Sound Negative by . . . . NT Audio
Negative Cutter . . Original Conforming Services
Color . . Technicolor Creative Services East Coast
Color Timer . . . . Fred Heid
Technicolor Coordinator . . . Joey Violante
Dolby Sound Consultant . . . . Matt Kunau
Digital Optical and Visual Effects by
. . . Technicolor Creative Services Toronto

VFX Producer . . . . Persis Reynolds
VFX Project Manager . Sarah Wormsbecher
Lead Inferno Artist . . . . Jason Snea
Digital Matte Painting . . Jordan Nieuwland
Inferno Compositor . . . . . . Dug Claxton
Shake Compositor . . . . Sean O'Hara
2K Scanning & Recording . Andrew Pascoe
Mike Ellis

Recorded at DBC Sound, Inc.

"Hot Cha Cha"
Written by Ramon E. Valdes
Performed by Bebo Valdes
Courtesy of Absolute Spain

"My Little Suede Shoes"
Written by Charlie Parker
Performed by Paul Smith Trio
Courtesy of Criterion Music Productions

"Cherry"
Written by Ray Gilbert and Donald Redman
Performed by Alan Paul
Courtesy of Peer-Southern Productions, Inc.

"Sugar (That Sugar Baby O'Mine)"
Written by Edna Alexander, Sidney Mitchell,
and Maceo Pinkard
Performed by Billie Holiday
Courtesy of Columbia Records by arrangement with Sony BMG Music Entertainment

"Rojo"
Written by Red Garland
Performed by Red Garland
Courtesy of Fantasy

"Paula's Nightmare"
Written by Paula Watson
Performed by Paula Watson
Courtesy of Tuff City Records / Night Train International
By arrangement with Ocean Park Music Group

"My Man is Gone"
Written by Jack Lauderdale
Performed by Emanon Trio
Courtesy of Tuff City Records / Night Train
International
By arrangement with Ocean Park Music Group

"Butcher Boy"
Traditional
Performed by Lilly Brothers
Courtesy of Prestige Folklore

"Easy to Remember"
Written by Richard Rodgers and Lorenz
Hart
Performed by John Coltrane
Courtesy of Verve Records under license
from
Universal Music Enterprises

Manitoba Co-Producer . . Eagle Vision Inc.

Shot on location in the province of Manitoba
with the participation of the Manitoba Film
and Video Production Tax Credit and the
British Columbia Production Services Tax
Credit

About the Contributors

Dan Futterman (Screenplay / Executive Producer) makes his screenwriting debut with *Capote*. As an actor, his films include *The Birdcage, Enough,* and *Urbania,* which was accepted into the Sundance Film Festival and for which he received Best Actor at the Seattle Film Festival.

Futterman has appeared on stage in New York in numerous productions, including *Angels in America, The Lights, A Fair Country, Dealer's Choice,* among others. He appeared as a series regular on the CBS show *Judging Amy* and has played a recurring character on *Will and Grace.* He has also made guest appearances on *Sex and the City* and *Homicide: Life on the Street,* where he met his future wife, Anya Epstein, a writer and producer of the show. She gave him advice and support during the writing of *Capote,* and when it was finished he sent it to his childhood friends Bennett Miller and Philip Seymour Hoffman.

Anya and Dan married in 2000, and make their home in Los Angeles with their four-year-old daughter. They've co-written a romantic comedy, *Finn at the Blue Line,* which they're developing with Debra Messing.

Bennett Miller (Director) made the acclaimed 1998 documentary-portrait *The Cruise,* about New York City tour guide Timothy "Speed" Levitch. The film garnered considerable critical praise and notable awards, including the top prize of the International Forum at the Berlin Film Festival and the Emmy Award. The film was released theatrically by Artisan Pictures and will soon be released on DVD by Lions Gate Films.

Miller met *Capote* screenwriter Dan Futterman when they were twelve years old and have been friends for the last twenty-five years. Miller and Futterman met Philip Seymour Hoffman while attending a 1984 summer theater program in Saratoga Springs, New York.

Miller is also an acclaimed director of television commercials. He is currently in post-production on his second documentary feature.

Gerald Clarke (Book) is the author of *Capote,* the acclaimed biography of Truman Capote. Considered the bible for anyone with a serious interest in the author, the 547-page book involved more than thirteen years of research, including a decade talking to Capote himself. Published by Simon & Schuster in 1988, *Capote* stayed on the *New York Times* bestseller list for thirteen weeks, a record for a literary biography.

Born in Los Angeles, Clarke graduated from Yale University, where he majored in English. After Yale, he traveled and studied in Europe for a year, then spent another year at Harvard Law School. Deciding that the law was not for him—and vice versa—he turned to journalism, working as a reporter for the *New Haven Journal-Courier* and the *Baltimore Sun,* then as a writer for *Time.* At *Time* he wrote about nearly everything, from American and world politics to show business and television. His specialty was profiles, and he interviewed figures from all walks—a lengthy list that includes Mae West, Daniel Patrick Moynihan, Elizabeth Taylor, Joseph Campbell, Rex Harrison, John Gielgud, Laurence Olivier, Claudette Colbert, Marshall McLuhan, Alfred Hitchcock, and George Lucas.

Clarke has also written for many other magazines, from *TV Guide* to *Architectural Digest,* for which he is now a contributor. It was his series on writers in *Esquire* and the *Atlantic*—Gore Vidal, Vladimir Nabokov, P. G. Wodehouse, Allen Ginsberg, and Truman Capote—that led to his biography of Capote.

Get Happy, Clarke's biography of Judy Garland, was published by Random House in 2000. Once again the book received rave reviews and landed on the *New York Times* bestseller list. More recently, Clarke edited a volume of Truman Capote's letters, *Too Brief a Treat.* It was published by Random House in 2004.

Clarke is currently writing his first novel, partly based on a real story of murder and terror in the Midwest.

HQ